*Key History
for Key Stage 3*

The Twentieth Century World

*Neil DeMarco and
Richard Radway*

Stanley Thornes (Publishers) Ltd

Designed and typeset by Hilary Norman
Illustrations by Barking Dog Art, Beverley Curl, Hardlines and Tim Smith
Cover artwork by Lee Montgomery, Beehive Illustration
Picture research by Julia Hanson

First published in 1995 by:
Stanley Thornes (Publishers) Ltd
Ellenborough House
Wellington Street
CHELTENHAM GL50 1YD
England

A catalogue record for this book is available from the British Library.

ISBN 0–7487–1932–6

Printed and bound in Hong Kong

Acknowledgements

The authors and publishers are grateful to the following for permission to reproduce illustrations and photographs in this book.

The Advertising Archives, 41 (top, left and right); AKG, 12 (top), 29, 31, 34 (left), 35 (top), 40, 57, 61; Barnaby's Picture Library, 78; British Library, 43 (bottom); Culver Pictures, 45, 90 (right); ET Archive, 27 (top); Hulton Deutsch Collection, 8, 25, 36, 52, 53, 86, 93; Illustrated London News, 51, 66; Imperial War Museum, 15, 16, 18, 21, 23 (top), 23 (bottom right), 24, 27 (bottom), 63, 65, 68, 69, 72, 76 (bottom), 77, 79; Japanese National Tourist Office, 90 (left); Mary Evans Picture Library, 73, 74, 76 (top); Moro, Rome, 30; NASA, 5, 89; National Portrait Gallery, 26; Peter Newark, 4, 34 (right), 38, 39, 41 (bottom), 42 (middle), 47, 62, 80 (top); Popperfoto, 67, 80 (bottom, left and right), 85, 88 (bottom), 95; Range Pictures, 42 (top), 43 (top); Reeve Photography, Cambridge, 88 (top); Rex Features, 87 (left); Robert Hunt, 7, 9, 12 (bottom), 35 (bottom), 70; Spectrum Colour Library, 87 (right); Staatslische Kunstammlungen, Dresden, 23 (bottom left); Ullstein Bilderdienst, 58; Visual Arts Library, 42 (bottom); Weidenfeld & Nicolson Archives, 46.

Every effort has been made to contact copyright holders and we apologise if any have been overlooked.

Contents

1 A world transformed

- **Which power has overtaken the European nations to dominate the world in the twentieth century?**
- **Which political ideas have been most important in the twentieth century?**
- **How has technology developed in the twentieth century?**

The world in 1900

When the twentieth century began, vast areas of the globe were ruled by Britain, France and Germany. These European **powers** had **colonies** throughout the world and together these colonies made up **empires** (see Source **A**). The British Empire had a population ten times that of Britain.

The emergence of the United States

In the eighteenth century the United States was a colony ruled by the British, but the Americans rebelled and broke away from Britain in 1776 to govern themselves. By 1900 the USA was already the wealthiest country in the world, producing more steel and coal than any other nation.

During the next 50 years, America added military might to economic strength to become the world's dominant power.

The end of Empires

After the Second World War the European empires began to break up.

The inhabitants of the colonies began to support a movement called **nationalism**, to break up these empires and rule themselves. India broke away from Britain in 1947 (Source **B**) and Kenya did the same in 1963. The empires of the other European countries, such as France and Portugal, also broke up. You can read more about this in the last chapter.

Source A The European colonial empires in 1900

Legend:
- British Empire
- German Empire
- French Empire

Source B During the First World War Indians volunteered to fight with Britain against Germany in defence of the British empire. Twenty years later they were demanding to leave that same empire. This cartoon from 1941 shows Indians driving out the British Prime Minister, Winston Churchill.

Communism

Many nationalists believed in the political ideas of **Communism**. Communists believed that colonies should overthrow their European rulers. They believed that workers should control the factories and the peasants should own the land – an idea that was especially popular in the poorer, mainly agricultural parts of the world.

Communist ideas did not go down well with factory owners and rich landowners. They preferred the system of **Capitalism**. Capitalists believe that factories and land should stay in the hands of private owners. The world's Communist and Capitalist countries have spent most of the twentieth century quarrelling with each other, but this conflict is less serious now that the world's first and most powerful Communist country, the Soviet Union, no longer believes in Communism. You can read more about Communism in Chapter 4.

A new world for women?

In 1900 women were still treated as second-class citizens in comparison with men. The role of women has changed since 1900. Women today can vote in elections in every country in Europe, but they have had to fight for this right. However, there are some countries in the world where this, and other basic rights, are still denied to women.

The First and Second World Wars played a major role in changing the attitudes to women and their role in society in Britain and elsewhere, as you will see in Chapter 9. In 1979 Margaret Thatcher became Britain's first woman Prime Minister, but today only about 5 per cent of British MPs are women.

Science and technology

In 1903 the world's first powered flight took place. It lasted just 59 seconds and covered 260 metres. Only 66 years later the first man set foot on the moon after a flight of 384,000 kilometers. Chapter 10 will help to explain how this tremendous transformation took place. The twentieth century has seen similar giant strides in many areas of science and technology such as medicine, communications, and weapons of war.

Source C The first man on the moon, 20 July 1969

Key words

Power   A dominant country.
Colony   A country ruled by another more powerful country.
Empire   A group of colonies under the control of another powerful nation.
Nationalism   A strong feeling of pride for one's country, especially the desire to free it from foreign control.

Communism   Based on the idea that the workers, and not just the rich, should control the economy. Communists believe that all the major businesses should be owned by the state and not by private individuals.
Capitalism   Based on the idea that factories and land work more efficiently if they are owned by private individuals and not the state.

Remember...

- The European nations are less powerful now than they were at the beginning of the twentieth century.

- The USA is now the world's greatest power.

- Communist and nationalist ideas have played a major role in changing the world in the twentieth century.

- The twentieth century has seen tremendous changes in space, military, medical and communications technologies.

Investigations

1 Which new power challenged the Europeans' dominance of the world?

2 Which two ideas helped to break up the European empires?

3 Why was Communism especially popular in the poorer parts of the world?

4 Why is the conflict between Communism and Capitalism less serious now?

5 Why are women in Britain still far from having a real influence in politics?

2 Europe at war

Great Power rivalry

Europe in the early twentieth century

In 1914 the first ever world war broke out. All the major countries of the world took part. Many people had been expecting a war for some time. Sources **A** and **B** help to explain why the First World War started.

Source A Europe in 1900

Ruled by Queen Victoria. Britain was Europe's leading industrial power, with an empire which included India, Australia and much of Africa. Britain needed a navy larger than any other, in order to defend this empire. The British therefore feared any other country which built up a large navy.

Ruled by Tsar Nicholas the Second. Russia had the largest population and the largest army in Europe. However, the army was poorly led and badly equipped. Russia wanted the Austro-Hungarian Empire to break up and replace it with one of their own.

A **republic**. France worked closely with Britain. Germany had taken the region of Alsace-Lorraine from France in 1871 and France wanted to take it back.

Ruled by Emperor Franz Josef. An Empire rather than a country. Many different nationalities lived in the Austro-Hungarian Empire. Many of them no longer wanted to be part of the empire. Among these were Serbs, who looked to Russia for support. Austria-Hungary wanted to dominate the **Balkans** to prevent its empire breaking up.

Ruled by Kaiser Wilhelm. Germany wanted to build a worldwide empire and so needed a large navy. A fast-growing industrial power, but still an important market for British manufactured goods. Allied to Italy and Austria-Hungary in the Triple **Alliance**.

A member of the Triple Alliance. Italy did not want to take part in wars involving its allies.

Ruled by a Sultan. Turkey had once dominated the Balkans but was now very weak.

GREAT BRITAIN

GERMANY

Alsace-Lorraine

RUSSIA

AUSTRIA-HUNGARY

FRANCE

ITALY

THE BALKANS

TURKEY

Key words

Republic A country ruled by an elected government rather than by a monarch. For example, Germany and the United States of America.
Alliance When two countries sign a treaty they form an alliance. They agree to help one another.

The treaty will describe what sort of help that will involve. When two countries join in an Alliance they are known as Allies.
Balkans An area of land in south-east Europe. Inhabited by many different nationalities, including Serbs.

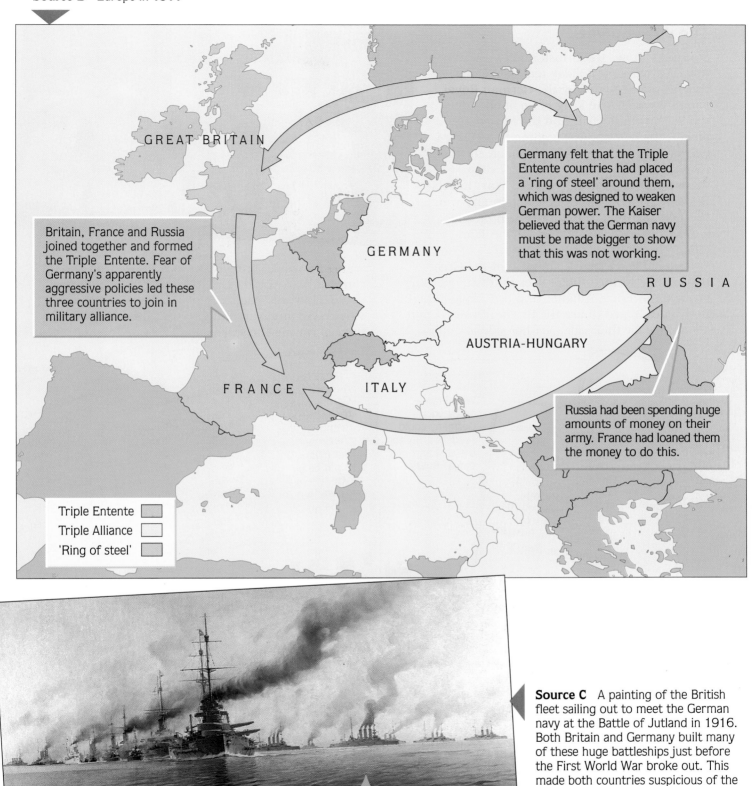

Germany felt that the Triple Entente countries had placed a 'ring of steel' around them, which was designed to weaken German power. The Kaiser believed that the German navy must be made bigger to show that this was not working.

Britain, France and Russia joined together and formed the Triple Entente. Fear of Germany's apparently aggressive policies led these three countries to join in military alliance.

GREAT BRITAIN

GERMANY

RUSSIA

AUSTRIA-HUNGARY

FRANCE

ITALY

Russia had been spending huge amounts of money on their army. France had loaned them the money to do this.

Triple Entente
Triple Alliance
'Ring of steel'

Source C A painting of the British fleet sailing out to meet the German navy at the Battle of Jutland in 1916. Both Britain and Germany built many of these huge battleships just before the First World War broke out. This made both countries suspicious of the other.

Investigations

1 Study Sources **A** and **B**. There were three main disputes in Europe in 1914:
   a) between England and Germany;
   b) between France and Germany;
   c) between Austria-Hungary and Russia.

Explain the reasons for each of these disputes.

The power game

Source **D** shows the British and Russian Royal Families on holiday together. Often they would be joined by the German Royal Family as well. The King of England (Edward the Seventh), the Tsar and the Kaiser were all cousins. Politics was a game to be played between them to gain an advantage for their own country. When the Russian Prime Minister, Kokovtzov, advised the Tsar that the Russian army would be defeated in any war, the Tsar told him to mind his own business. Foreign policy was a matter for the Tsar alone.

Source **B** on page 7 shows that the Great Powers had formed themselves into two opposing groups: the Triple Alliance and the Triple Entente. Both sides hoped to use the threat of war to gain advantage for their side. Neither side actually

Source D The British and Russian Royal Families at Cowes, Isle of Wight, in 1909

wanted a war to break out. They hoped that the *threat* of war would cause the other side to back down. However, each side was certain that they would win any war, and so both sides were willing to keep raising the stakes.

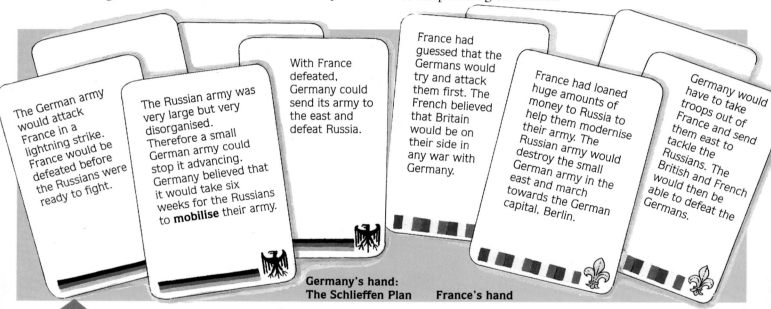

The German army would attack France in a lightning strike. France would be defeated before the Russians were ready to fight.

The Russian army was very large but very disorganised. Therefore a small German army could stop it advancing. Germany believed that it would take six weeks for the Russians to **mobilise** their army.

With France defeated, Germany could send its army to the east and defeat Russia.

Germany's hand: The Schlieffen Plan

France had guessed that the Germans would try and attack them first. The French believed that Britain would be on their side in any war with Germany.

France had loaned huge amounts of money to Russia to help them modernise their army. The Russian army would destroy the small German army in the east and march towards the German capital, Berlin.

Germany would have to take troops out of France and send them east to tackle the Russians. The British and French would then be able to defeat the Germans.

France's hand

Source E The Great Power Poker Game. Poker is a game of bluff. The aim is to keep raising the stakes to convince your opponent that he cannot win and so will back down.

It seemed that war was now inevitable, since both sides were so sure that they would win if war were to break out. Europe held its breath and waited.

Remember…

- **The war was caused by the diplomatic game being played by the Great Powers.**
- **France and Germany were willing to risk fighting a war, because they both believed they would win.**

Key words

Mobilise Bringing all troops, including part-time soldiers, into active service. In the case of Russia this could create an army of 6 million men.

Investigations

1 In your own words explain how the Schlieffen Plan would lead to a German victory in a war with France.

2 You are France. How would you react as Germany keeps raising the stakes by building more and more battleships?

3 France raises the stakes by giving more money to Russia. Why do you think that Germany did not believe that this would be important?

The outbreak of war

Why did war break out in 1914?
Was Germany to blame for the outbreak of the war?

Source A The Balkans

Austro-German Empire, made up of many nationalities. Feared that Slav people would want the chance to join Serbia.

The Russian Empire containing many nationalities, including Slavs. Russia wanted to dominate the Balkans.

In Bosnia and Montenegro the majority of the population were Slavs. Ruled by Turkey until 1908. Invaded by Austria-Hungary in 1908 to prevent moves towards Slav independence.

RUSSIA

AUSTRIA-HUNGARY

ROMANIA

BOSNIA

SERBIA

Black Sea

MONTENEGRO

BULGARIA

TURKEY IN EUROPE

TURKEY

GREECE

Ruled by Turkey but made up of people of many nationalities, including Slavs and Greeks. Encouraged by Russia, Serbia, Bulgaria and Greece attacked Turkey in 1912, conquering must of Turkey in Europe.

Source B Archduke Franz Ferdinand and his wife Sophie in their car touring Sarajevo in June, 1914. You can see how easy it was for Princip to shoot them once the car had stopped.

Source C
From the front page of a British newspaper

Daily

NO. 4,438.   LOND

HEIR TO AUSTRIAN THRONE MURDERED.

ARCHDUKE AND HIS WIFE SHOT DEAD IN THE STREET.

DETERMINED PLOT.

BOMB FIRST THROWN AT THEIR CAR.

SECOND ATTEMPT WITHIN AN HOUR.

BOY ASSASSIN.

MURDERED ARCHDU
The Archduke Francis Ferdinand and

the burgomaster and the members of the town council, and it was clear to all that he was then in a furious temper, and bitterly resentful of what had happened.
The burgomaster stepped forward to

Investigations Look at Source **C**. Does the newspaper seem worried about the possibility of war? Give reasons for your answer.

9

The assassination of Franz Ferdinand

On 28 June 1914 the Archduke Franz Ferdinand visited the Bosnian capital of Sarajevo with his wife, Sophie. It was their wedding anniversary and he was the heir to the throne of Austria-Hungary. As his four-car convoy drove through the streets of Sarajevo, a local Serb, Cabrinovic, tried to assassinate the Archduke with a hand grenade. He missed, but twenty onlookers were injured.

Franz Ferdinand decided that he would visit the injured in hospital, but the car's driver at first continued on the original route. He was ordered to stop and reverse. In doing so he slowed down alongside Gavrilo Princip. He was a Serbian member of the Black Hand gang, who wanted to free Bosnia from Austrian control. Princip leapt onto the car and fired a gun at the Archduke and his wife, who both died soon afterwards.

Why did Sarajevo lead to war?

The Archduke was not greatly loved in Austria-Hungary and there was little public mourning at his death. However, Austria-Hungary was determined to destroy the power of Serbia which had grown so much in the previous two years. On 28 July the Austro-Hungarian Empire declared war on Serbia. Austria's ally, Germany, warned Russia not to get involved in defence of the Serbs. However, the Russians decided to mobilise their army. It was this action which led to war.

Look back at the Schlieffen Plan (Germany's hand in the Poker Game in Source **E** on p.8). Russian mobilisation meant that it would not be long before the Russian army was marching towards Berlin. The Schlieffen Plan required France to be defeated before the Russians were attacked. The Germans therefore had to launch an attack on the French as soon as possible. The best way to do this was to attack through Belgium, even though this was likely to bring Britain into the war, since Britain had made a treaty with Belgium.

Did Germany start the war?

At the end of the war all the countries who had fought against Germany were agreed that Germany had started the war. They even put a 'War Guilt Clause' in the final treaty so that it was officially declared that the war was Germany's fault and that they would have to pay for all of the damage caused by the armies of both sides. Was this fair?

> In order to protect German trade and commerce under existing conditions, only one thing will suffice, namely, Germany must possess a battle fleet of such strength that even for the most powerful naval adversary, a war would involve such risks as to make that power's own supremacy doubtful.

Source D From the German Navy Law, 1900

Source E By the British historian L. Turner, writing in 1970

> In December 1909 the *Daily Mail* published a series of articles on 'England and Germany', which declared that Germany was aiming at 'world domination' and 'cold-bloodedly' preparing to destroy the British Empire.

From L. Turner, *The Origins of the First World War*, 1970

Investigations

1 Explain how the Russian mobilisation led to war.

2 Copy the table below into your exercise book. Look at Sources **A** and **B** on pages 6–7 and at Sources **D** and **E** on this page. Can you find any evidence in these sources to suggest that Germany was to blame for starting the First World War? Write this evidence in the appropriate box.

3 Now look at these sources again. Can you find any evidence that other countries may have helped to start the war? Put this evidence in your table.

4 Do you believe that it was fair to blame Germany for starting the war? Give your reasons, using the information you have put in your table.

Remember...

- War broke out in 1914 when the Austro-Hungarian Empire declared war on Serbia, following the assassination of Archduke Franz Ferdinand in Sarajevo.

- Germany was not the only country responsible for starting the war.

Source	Evidence that Germany was to blame	Evidence that other countries were to blame
A (page 6)		
B (page 7)		
D		
E		

Battlefronts on land and sea

The war on land

At first it looked as though the Schlieffen Plan would work. The German army invaded Belgium but their progress was slower than expected as they were held back by the British army at Mons. Although the Germans won the battle, the British retreated in to France, slowing down the German advance.

Just ten days into the war the Russians invaded Germany and so the Germans had to send soldiers to fight the Russians in the east. This meant that there were now fewer German troops to fight the British and the French. The retreating British joined up with the French at the river Marne, to the west of Paris. Here, six days of fierce fighting led to a German retreat.

The Schlieffen Plan had failed. A new war had now begun. General von Moltke is supposed to have told the Kaiser 'Germany has lost the war'. The Germans retreated to ground that was easier to defend and dug themselves in. The British and French also dug themselves into trenches facing the Germans. In any line of battle, whether or not trenches are used, each side will try to get around the ends of the line to surround the enemy. In this case, both sides were forced to extend their lines to natural barriers, the coast of Belgium in the north and the borders of Switzerland in the south, to prevent this happening.

Source A Battlefronts of the war

1916. The Battle of Jutland. The only major battle between the British and German fleets.

1914. Germany invades France through Belgium. British and French counter-attack leads to the Western Front, stretching from the English Channel to Switzerland.

Russian attacks are successful at first, but Germany finally forces Russia out of the war.

Although a member of the Triple Alliance, Italy does not join the war in 1914. In 1915 Italy joins Britain and France.

1915. Britain tries to defeat Turkey and Austria-Hungary by attacking Gallipoli. It is a terrible failure.

GREAT BRITAIN

RUSSIA

GERMANY

BELGIUM

FRANCE

SWITZERLAND

AUSTRIA-HUNGARY

ITALY

SERBIA

TURKEY

The war in the east

The Germans had expected that it would take six weeks for the Russians to mobilise their army. It took ten days. The Germans were forced to abandon the Schlieffen Plan and send more men to fight the Russians. In two huge battles – Tannenburg and the Masurian Lakes – the Russian army suffered appalling losses. Although they had an army of six million, they could not produce enough weapons or equipment to arm them properly.

From 1915 onwards the Germans penetrated deep into Russian territory. In February 1917 there was a revolution in Russia which overthrew the Tsar. In October a second revolution resulted in a take-over by the Communists and their leader, Lenin. They took Russia out of the war. This meant that the Germans could transfer their army back to the west.

The war at sea

The threat of a huge German navy had played an important part in creating the alliances which led to the outbreak of war. Yet the two navies played little part in the fighting. Both sides had spent so much money in building up their navies that they did not want to risk losing them, and without a navy each side would be open to invasion.

The Battle of Jutland

The only major sea battle took place on 31 May 1916 at Jutland in the North Sea (see Source **C** on page 7). A total of 259 warships were involved in the battle. The Germans inflicted the most damage and so claimed victory. However, the German navy remained in port for the rest of the war and so the British claimed the overall success. The British navy was therefore free to patrol the seas and so blockade Germany, preventing much-needed food and raw materials from being imported. These shortages were to play an important part in Germany's decision to end the war in November 1918.

U-boats

Britain imported most of its food during the war. In an attempt to starve the British into submission, the Germans used submarines – 'U-boats' – to sink merchant ships bringing supplies to Britain. It was almost successful. In April 1917 Britain had only six weeks' supply of food left.

Source B By the end of 1916 the number of Russian casualties had reached the horrifying figure of five million. Not surprisingly, many Russians wanted the war to end.

The success of the U-boats was double-edged. By sinking neutral ships which might be bringing supplies to Britain, the Germans greatly angered the USA. In 1917 America decided to join the war and fight against Germany.

The Western Front

The war became a static **war of attrition**. Source **E** highlights the major battles which tried to end the stalemate. Eventually it was the American army which decided the outcome. Although the USA entered the war in 1917 their troops did not reach Europe in large numbers until 1918. Both sides had by now lost all their best fighting men and the Germans were having to use men considered too young or too old to fight in the earlier stages of the war. In contrast the British and the French dead were now being replaced by fit, young, well-equipped Americans.

Source C German U-boats in the port of Kiel. First World War submarines were very small and yet they achieved much greater success than the huge battleships.

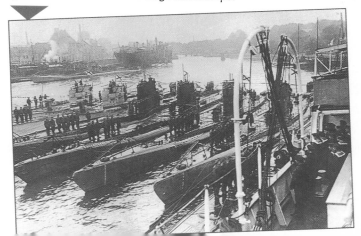

British destroyers and torpedo boats armed with torpedoes and depth charges. Both weapons could sink U-boats. By the end of 1917 one in four U-boats was being sunk.

British naval ships created a smoke-screen so that the convoy was invisible to U-boats when they came to the surface. There was no radar, so sight was the only way to find the convoy.

Merchant ships painted in camouflage colours to break up their outline and make them difficult to see.

Merchant ships

British destroyers and torpedo boats

Source D The convoy system. The British Prime Minister, Lloyd George, introduced this against attack from U-boats. It more than halved British losses within a few months.

In March 1918 the Germans launched one final attack, before too many Americans had joined the war. At first it was very successful and it pushed the Allies back to the Somme. However, by August large numbers of Americans had arrived and the advance was halted. The Germans knew that they could not replace their casualties and in November they finally surrendered to the Allies.

Source E Map of the Western Front 1915–17

German

Ypres

British

Somme

THE WESTERN FRONT

Switzerland

Ypres was in a salient – a piece of land which stuck out into enemy territory. It offered the British a chance to get behind the enemy lines, so the Germans wanted to capture it. There were four great battles here. At the third, in 1917, the British tried to break out but lost 250,000 men and only advanced 800 yards.

The Battle of the Somme, July – November 1916 The British launched an attack, partly to draw German soldiers away from Verdun and partly to try and break through the German lines. The casualties were even worse than Verdun.

Verdun 1916 The Germans tried to bleed France dry. They hoped that so many French soldiers would die defending Verdun that the French would be forced to surrender.

Remember...

- **The Allies won the war because the USA could supply them with fresh troops and because the blockade by the British navy was starving Germany of food and supplies.**

Key words

War of attrition This means wearing the other side down by killing so many men that they could not be replaced. This is exactly what took place at Verdun and on the Somme.

Investigations

1 Why do you think von Moltke believed that Germany had lost the war after their defeat at the Battle of the Marne?

2 What was the purpose of the German attack on Verdun?

3 Why is the success of the U-boats described as 'double-edged'?

4 Look at Source **D**. Explain how the convoy system protected merchant ships from U-boat attack.

3 Depth Study: The Western Front

'Hell cannot be so terrible'

No Man's Land

Shortly before he was killed, a French infantry officer, Alfred Joubaire, wrote in his diary 'What scenes of horror and carnage!...Hell cannot be so terrible. Man is mad!' When the war broke out in August 1914 no one realised that it would be so horrific. Most people thought that it would 'all be over by Christmas'.

In fact by the start of 1915 millions of men were dug into trenches facing each other across **No Man's Land**. The generals of both sides had expected a war in which their armies would move quickly. They had not expected to have to dig below ground in order to be safe.

Source A The Front Line

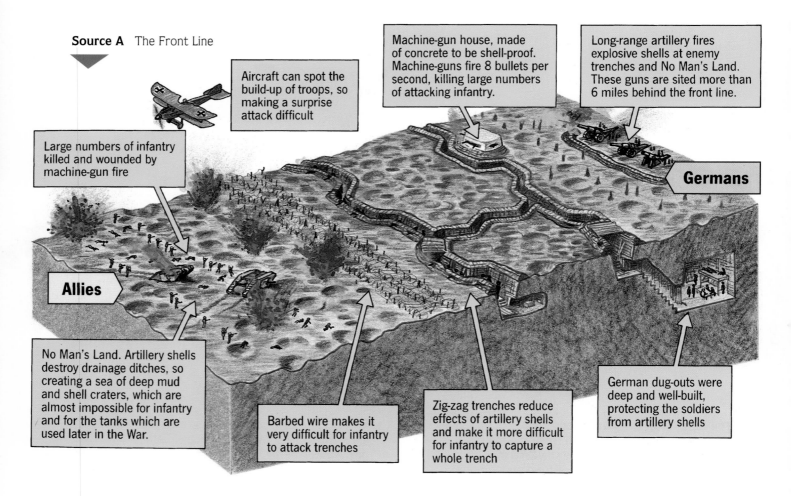

Aircraft can spot the build-up of troops, so making a surprise attack difficult

Machine-gun house, made of concrete to be shell-proof. Machine-guns fire 8 bullets per second, killing large numbers of attacking infantry.

Long-range artillery fires explosive shells at enemy trenches and No Man's Land. These guns are sited more than 6 miles behind the front line.

Large numbers of infantry killed and wounded by machine-gun fire

Germans

Allies

No Man's Land. Artillery shells destroy drainage ditches, so creating a sea of deep mud and shell craters, which are almost impossible for infantry and for the tanks which are used later in the War.

Barbed wire makes it very difficult for infantry to attack trenches

Zig-zag trenches reduce effects of artillery shells and make it more difficult for infantry to capture a whole trench

German dug-outs were deep and well-built, protecting the soldiers from artillery shells

Key words

No Man's Land The name given to the strip of land between the opposing front-line trenches. See Source **A**.

Stalemate A standstill, when neither side was in a strong enough position to defeat the other.

Trench warfare

In the early stages of the war the Germans had attacked with great speed and taken control of much of Belgium and parts of northern France. This meant that the British, French and Belgian armies had to push them out. This had three important results:

1 The Allies had to attack the German trenches.
2 The Germans were able to choose the higher ground which was easier to defend.
3 The Germans were able to make their trenches and dug-outs very strong since they intended to remain exactly where they were.

As the sources show, it was very difficult for the Allies to attack and capture the German positions, so a stalemate developed.

Source C What a soldier had to carry in the trenches

Each man carried 66 lbs [29 kgs] – over half his body weight – which made it difficult to get out of a trench, impossible to move quicker than at a slow walk or to rise or lay down quickly.

From *History of the First World War* by Liddell Hart, written in 1972

Source B A description of the conditions in which soldiers had to fight

Ironically one of the men's most valuable protections, the greatcoat, could prove a dreadful liability in wet weather. The coats weighed approximately 7 lbs [3 kgs]...It was quite common for the combination of mud and water to amount to an extra 34 lbs [15 kgs] and one officer reported that when the greatcoats of a platoon coming out of the Somme trenches were weighed, one of them was actually 58 lbs [26 kgs].

From *Eye Deep in Hell* by John Ellis, written in 1976

Source D By Seaman Joseph Murray, who took part in the attack on Beaumont Hamel on 13 November 1916

There were 12 or 13 rows of barbed wire in front of the first trench and when the bombardment goes into that it's supposed to cut it, but it doesn't destroy the wire, it builds into a bloody heap with gaps in it here and there and, when the enemy's alive and awake to the idea you're coming, they've got their machine-guns trained on these gaps – therefore you get slaughtered.

Quoted in *The Somme* by Lyn MacDonald, 1983

Source E Trench warfare

Investigations

1 Look at Source **A**. Make a list of all the information you can find which helps to explain why it was so difficult for each side to attack.

2 Look at Sources **B**, **C** and **D**. Add to your list any further information that you can find in these sources.

3 Decide which are the three most important reasons why a stalemate developed. Explain how each made it likely that any attack would fail.

Remember...

- The trenches on both sides were so well defended it was virtually impossible to break through. The result was a stalemate.

New weapons

Gas

Generals on both sides were desperate to break the stalemate. Both sides relied on heavy **artillery** bombardment to try to destroy the enemy's defences and to follow this up by sending wave upon wave of **infantry** 'over the top' to cross No Man's Land and capture the enemy trenches. This resulted in heavy casualties. Both sides tried to develop new weapons which would achieve a breakthrough.

The Germans developed poison gas as their secret weapon. It was first used near Ypres on 22 April 1915. The effect was devastating. Cylinders full of chlorine gas were brought to the front and opened as soon as the wind was blowing towards the British and French lines. Soon troops were fleeing from their trenches. Chlorine irritates the lining of the lungs when it is breathed in, and the irritation produces liquid in the lungs. If enough liquid is breathed in, the person will drown.

However, the British soon developed gas masks which offered some protection, both against chlorine and another gas called phosgene, which the British correctly guessed that the Germans would eventually use. Although these could be penetrated by heavy doses of gas, only 3 per cent of casualties in a gas attack actually died, showing that gas was not the breakthrough weapon. Indeed when the British did the same and used chlorine against the Germans at Loos on 25 September 1915, it revealed many of the disadvantages of poison gas. The wind was not strong enough and many British troops were poisoned in their own trenches. Some cylinders were hit by enemy artillery, bursting open and poisoning everyone around.

Later in the war both sides put liquid gas into artillery shells which could then be fired into enemy trenches. This was much more effective and, even if wearing gas masks, it could force defenders to abandon a front-line trench.

The tank

Source A   A tank bogged down in a shell crater, 1917

As early as January 1915 Winston Churchill wrote to the Prime Minister, Asquith, complaining that the British Generals had not thought up any ideas to break through the enemy trenches (Source **B**). He believed that the tank would be the weapon to win the war.

> The question to be solved is…the actual getting across 100 or 200 yards of open space and wire entanglements…All this was apparent two months ago but no steps have been taken and no preparations made. It would be quite easy in a short time to fit up a number of steam tractors with small armoured shelters, in which men and machine-guns could be placed, which would be bullet-proof. Forty or fifty of these machines prepared secretly and brought into position at nightfall could advance quite certainly into the enemy's trenches with their machine-gun fire.
>
> **Quoted in *The Last Great Battle of the Somme* by Cheyne**

Source B   Winston Churchill, 5 January 1915

The British did develop tanks. Instead of wheels they used caterpillar tracks developed in the Canadian logging industry. These spread the weight of the tank over a wide area so allowing it to travel over uneven and muddy ground. Their strange shape allowed them to cross trenches as is shown in Source **C**.

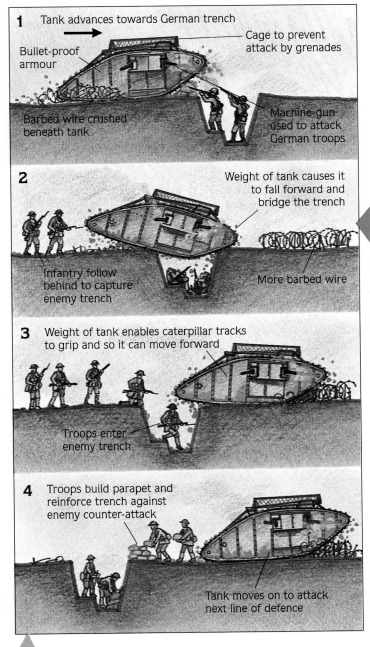

1 Tank advances towards German trench

Bullet-proof armour

Cage to prevent attack by grenades

Barbed wire crushed beneath tank

Machine-gun used to attack German troops

2 Weight of tank causes it to fall forward and bridge the trench

Infantry follow behind to capture enemy trench

More barbed wire

3 Weight of tank enables caterpillar tracks to grip and so it can move forward

Troops enter enemy trench

4 Troops build parapet and reinforce trench against enemy counter-attack

Tank moves on to attack next line of defence

Tanks were first used on the Somme on 15 September 1916. However, of the 49 tanks to be used in this battle, only 9 reached the German trenches. Most simply broke down while others stuck in the mud and the shell craters created by the heavy British artillery bombardment. The tanks weighed 28 tonnes, so that even with caterpillar tracks they still sank into the soft mud. At the Battle of the Somme their average speed was half a mile per hour. This meant that they were an easy target for German artillery. Once hit by a shell they simply became a fiery tomb for the eight men inside.

The first great success for the tank came in 1917 at Cambrai when they enabled British troops to make a major advance. This time there had been no artillery bombardment and so the ground was firm. However, with German trenches captured and open territory in front of them, the attack had to stop because most of the tanks needed repairing.

Source C   How a tank crossed an enemy trench

I t was marvellous…The tank waddled on with its guns blazing and we could see Jerry popping up and down, not knowing what to do, whether to stay or run…The Jerries waited until our tank was only a few yards away and then fled – or hoped to! The tank just shot them down and the machine-gun post, the gun itself, the dead and the wounded who hadn't been able to run, just disappeared. The tank went right over them. We would have danced for joy if it had been possible out there.

Quoted in *The Somme* by Lyn MacDonald

Source D   By Lance Corporal Len Lovell, an eye-witness to the first use of tanks on 15 September

Investigations

1 Read Source **D**. What evidence does it provide about the effect of the tank on the morale of British troops?

2 What evidence does Source **D** provide about the effect of tanks on the morale of German troops?

3 What has happened to the tank in Source **A**? Why did this tend to happen to tanks?

4 Were tanks as successful as Churchill hoped? Explain your answer.

5 Write your own 'Remember' box for this unit. Did the new weapons help to break the stalemate?

Key words

Artillery   Large guns which fired shells over a large distance, and so could be positioned well behind the front line.
Infantry   Soldiers fighting on foot.

A battle in focus: The Battle of the Somme

We have looked in general at how First World War battles were fought. Now we will look at perhaps the most dramatic battle in the whole war, the Battle of the Somme, which was fought in the summer and autumn of 1916. If you turn back to Source **E** page 13 you can see where and why the British decided to launch the attack which began this battle.

The plan was to attack a 30 km stretch of German trenches – the most strongly defended on the whole Western Front. In the ten days before the attack the British artillery had rained an unbelievable 1 732 873 shells on the German trenches – a bombardment so great it could be heard in England. The bombardment was made up of high explosive shells to kill German troops and **shrapnel** shells to cut the German barbed wire.

1 July 1916: the attack

At 'zero hour', 7.30 a.m., nearly 100 000 British troops climbed out of their trenches and walked towards the German front line. The British artillery was ordered to remain silent for ten minutes to allow the soldiers to cross No Man's Land without being shelled by their own side.

But something had gone badly wrong. Machine-gun fire ripped into the advancing British troops. The British bombardment had not killed the German soldiers who had been sheltering in very deep and well-built dug-outs and tunnels.

To make matters worse, the seven-day bombardment had turned No Man's Land into a sea of shell craters, which made it even more difficult for the British troops to cross it. The shrapnel had failed to break the German wire. In fact the explosive shells had often caused it to become tangled and utterly impassable.

On 1 July the British army suffered the worst ever casualties in its entire history. Over 20 000 soldiers were killed or missing and over 34 000 wounded.

Source A
The entrance to a German dug-out on the Somme

Beaumont Hamel

At 7.20 a.m. a mine containing over 40 000 pounds of explosive was detonated under the Hawthorn Redoubt, the German machine-gun position which overlooked this part of the front line. The photograph of the explosion (Source **B**) was taken as it happened. It looks like a success, but it was not. Many German soldiers were killed in the explosion, but by 'zero hour' – 7.30 a.m. – reserve soldiers had moved machine-guns to the edge of the crater caused by the explosion, and fired on the British attack.

By the end of the day, 1800 troops from Britain and the Empire were killed. A further 3 000 were wounded. Out of 800 reserve troops from the Canadian island of Newfoundland, 710 were killed or wounded.

At Beaumont Hamel you can still visit a small part of the Somme battlefield which has been preserved.

Source B 7.20 a.m., 1 July 1916. This photograph shows a British mine destroying the Hawthorn Redoubt

Key words

Shrapnel A shell full of small lead pellets, which would explode above ground level, sending a shower of pellets in all directions.

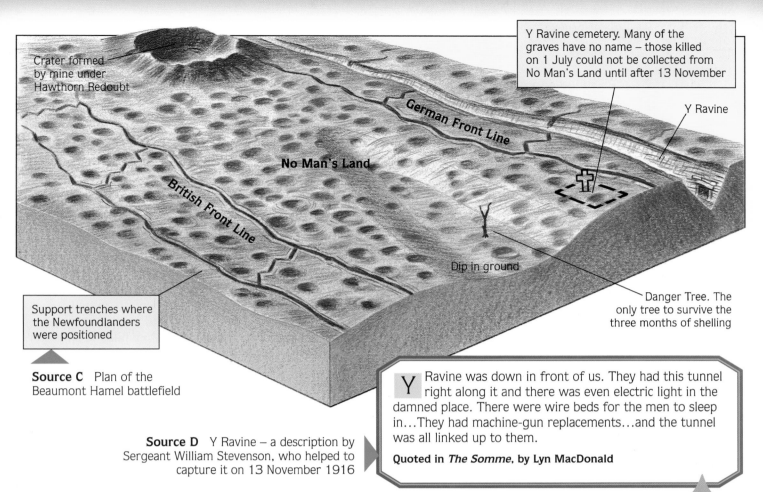

Crater formed by mine under Hawthorn Redoubt

German Front Line

Y Ravine cemetery. Many of the graves have no name – those killed on 1 July could not be collected from No Man's Land until after 13 November

Y Ravine

No Man's Land

British Front Line

Dip in ground

Danger Tree. The only tree to survive the three months of shelling

Support trenches where the Newfoundlanders were positioned

Source C Plan of the Beaumont Hamel battlefield

Source D Y Ravine – a description by Sergeant William Stevenson, who helped to capture it on 13 November 1916

Y Ravine was down in front of us. They had this tunnel right along it and there was even electric light in the damned place. There were wire beds for the men to sleep in…They had machine-gun replacements…and the tunnel was all linked up to them.

Quoted in *The Somme*, by Lyn MacDonald

13 November 1916

In the three months after 1 July 1916 the British continued to attack and gradually capture the German positions on the German front, and continued to suffer huge casualties. It was on 13 November 1916 that the last attack of the Battle of the Somme took place and Beaumont Hamel was finally captured.

Again, a mine was placed under the Hawthorn Redoubt, but this time it was detonated as the attack began. This time 'zero hour', the time of the attack, was 5.45 a.m.. This was 90 minutes before dawn, so the Germans would not be able to see the attackers.

This time the Germans were not ready and waiting. For the past month the British had been firing an artillery barrage at the German lines at 5.45 a.m. each morning. Therefore the Germans sheltered in their dug-outs, thinking that 13 November was to be just like the other mornings. Also huge numbers of shells full of the deadly poison gas phosgene mixed with chlorine were fired into Y Ravine to make sure the troops there could not join the battle. By the end of the day Beaumont Hamel was in British hands. This time the British casualties were less than half those on 1 July, although 2 200 soldiers lost their lives.

Remember…

- **The Battle of the Somme shows how the attacking tactics, although eventually successful, produced huge numbers of casualties.**

Investigations

1 Copy the table below.

	1 July	13 November
Time of 'zero hour'		
Artillery barrage		
Time of exploding Hawthorn mine		
Point at which troops started the attack		

For each item explain what happened on 1 July and 13 November, writing your answers in the correct column.

2 Explain how each of these four differences helped to give victory to the British on 13 November.

3 Of these differences, which do you feel was the most important in bringing victory to the British? Explain your answer.

Life in the trenches

What was it like to live and fight in the trenches?

✦ Trench systems
The Western Front did not simply consist of two front-line trenches facing each other across No Man's Land. Behind the front line were three or four roughly parallel lines of trenches, 100 metres or more apart.

Conditions in the trenches

What were the trenches like? Source **B** shows a cross-section of a trench. As shown in Source **C**, some of the trenches at Vimy Ridge have been reconstructed in concrete as a memorial to the men who died in them. However, they only tell part of the story.

Mud and water

Conditions in the trenches were very bad. The mud was often deep. At Ypres the German trenches were on higher ground, and so drainage channels were cut which sent the water down into the British trenches, which became very muddy whenever it rained. Trenches became full of water and mud. Sandbags lining the trenches collapsed as they filled with water and then the sides of the trenches gave way.

Source A Plan of British trench system

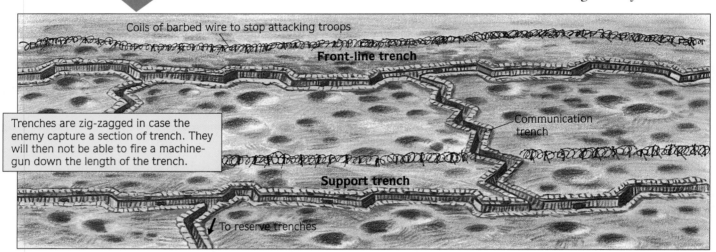

Coils of barbed wire to stop attacking troops

Front-line trench

Communication trench

Trenches are zig-zagged in case the enemy capture a section of trench. They will then not be able to fire a machine-gun down the length of the trench.

Support trench

↙ To reserve trenches

Source B Cross-section sketch of a trench

Source C Section of reconstructed trench at Vimy Ridge

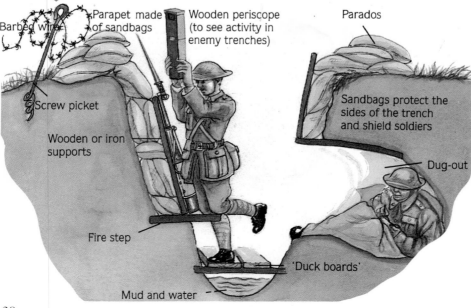

Barbed wire

Parapet made of sandbags

Wooden periscope (to see activity in enemy trenches)

Parados

Screw picket

Wooden or iron supports

Sandbags protect the sides of the trench and shield soldiers

Dug-out

Fire step

'Duck boards'

Mud and water

Source D A section of British trenches during the Battle of the Somme

Trenches were constantly shelled by enemy artillery, which smashed the sandbags and the sides of the trenches.

Illness and disease

The men had to live in the trenches. The only protection from the weather were dug-outs. The soldiers in Source **E** are resting in dug-outs. The men might spend days standing in mud. This could produce a disease called trench foot. To stop this spreading, the men had to rub whale oil onto their feet every day. Some men wanted to get trench foot so that they would be sent home. Therefore it was often the job of the man next to you to put on the whale oil, to make sure it was done. During the war over 74 000 men were admitted to hospital with trench foot.

Source E A British trench during the Battle of the Somme

There were other problems. The soldiers' clothes became infested with **lice**, so that the soldiers were soon covered in small bites. Clothing was deloused when it was sent to the laundry, but this only killed the lice, not their eggs. Lice were more than a discomfort. They also carried a disease known as trench fever. This did not kill, but meant up to three months off duty. It was not until 1918 that it was realised that the lice were the cause of this fever.

Source F Mark Plowman, a British soldier, describes the trenches on the Somme in 1916

Rats

Even more disturbing were the rats which ate the corpses lying in No Man's Land and in the trenches, as well as any food scraps they could find. There were probably tens of millions of rats along the Western Front. A Canadian soldier recalled that they were 'huge rats, so big that they would eat a wounded man if he couldn't defend himself'. If this seems unbelievable, remember that after a battle wounded men were too weak to move. The rats also brought disease – luckily not the plague, but a form of jaundice.

> The mud makes it all but impassable, and now that I have sunk in it up to the knees, I have a momentary terror of never being able to pull myself out. Such horror gives frenzied energy and I tear my legs free and go on. Little or no work is done for the simple reason that God has not yet constructed men able to make or repair trenches when the earth at every step holds them immobile.
>
> **Taken from** *Eye Deep in Hell*, **by John Ellis**

Investigations

Look at Sources **B** and **C** and then Sources **D** and **E**.

1 What can you find in Sources **D** and **E** which is not shown in Source **A**?

2 What aspects of a trench are not shown in any of these four sources?

3 Which two sources do you think tell you the most about what a trench was like – **B** and **C** or **D** and **E**? Give your reasons.

Key words

Lice Insects which live on humans in unclean conditions.

Repairing and guarding the trenches

Trenches needed regular repair to put right the damage from artillery shells. Sheets of galvanised iron or wooden boards could be used to support the sides. Replacing sections of broken barbed wire was dangerous. This was done at night since it meant leaving the trench. Even at night enemy snipers were alert and flares would be sent used to reveal the wire repairers.

Perhaps most dangerous of all was sentry duty. The enemy trenches had to be watched in case there was a surprise attack. Sentries stood in the trench with their head and soldiers above the **parapet**. This was because enemy snipers aimed at the top of the parapet, and a bullet through the chest was less likely to kill than one through the head!

The soldiers' view

You might expect all the men who fought in the First World War to feel the same way about what they had experienced. This was not the case, as you can see when you read Sources **G** to **J**.

Source G The opinion of Corporal Harry Shaw, a soldier in the war

> Whatever was gained, it wasn't worth the price that men paid to gain that advantage…It was just sheer bloody murder.
>
> **Quoted in *The Somme*, by Lyn MacDonald**

Source H Corporal Jack Beament, a soldier in the war, describes his reaction to the sight of dead British soldiers and to the horror around him

> A shell must have got them. There were bodies all around. You can't describe it. That massacre must have happened fourteen days before we got there. It was horrifying. We were all about twenty years of age and you're a bit callous then…You have no sort of feeling.
>
> **Quoted in *The Somme*, by Lyn MacDonald**

Source I By Bert Chaney, an 18 year-old who joined up on 4 August 1914. He arrived in France on 17 March 1915, although he did not write this until over 50 years later.

> Buttons, badges and boots highly polished, we swaggered down the hill, everyone in perfect step. We'd show these Frenchmen what a London Terrier Regiment was like. Now we had arrived in France the war was as good as over, or so we thought.
>
> **Quoted in M. Moynihan *People at War, 1914–18*, 1973**

Source J A soldier describes the comradeship in the trenches

> To live amongst men who would give their last fag, their last bite, aye, even their last breath if need be for a pal – that is comradeship, the comradeship of the trenches.
>
> **Quoted in *Eye Deep in Hell*, by John Ellis**

Remember...

- **Conditions in the trenches were terrible, and very dangerous.**
- **Bad conditions in the trenches led to illness and disease.**

Key words

Parapet Raised bank of sandbags in front of a trench (see Source **B** on page 20).

Investigations

1 Read Source **F** on page 21. What does it tell you about life in a trench which is not shown in Sources **D** and **E**?

2 In trying to find out what trench life was like, do you think a photograph like Source **E** (page 21) is more or less useful than a soldier's own account like Source **F**? Explain your answer.

3 What do Corporal Shaw and Corporal Beament feel about the war?

4 How can you explain that the soldiers in Sources **I** and **J** do not appear to feel the same way about the war as Shaw and Beament?

Focus Study: 'The Sorrowful Dark of Hell' – Art and poetry in the First World War

What does the art and poetry of the First World War tell us about the experiences and feelings of the soldiers who fought?

Art in the First World War

Source A The Menin Road, near Ypres in Belgium, painted by Paul Nash in 1919

Source C Stretchers pulled by mules bringing wounded to a **dressing station**, painted in 1919 by Stanley Spencer. Spencer was a member of the Royal Army Medical Corps during the war and was sent to northern Greece, which is why the soldiers in this picture are wearing cloth to protect their necks from the sun.

Source B *The War* by Otto Dix

Key words

Dressing station A dressing station was a medical point close to the front line. The wounded would be bandaged and receive emergency treatment before being taken to field hospitals behind the lines.

Wilfred Owen (Source **J** and **K**) spent the winter of 1916–7 on the front line but was then sent home on sick leave. He returned to the front on 1 September 1918 and was killed on 4 November, just seven days before the war ended. Sassoon and Owen both became famous because of their poetry about the war.

Source K   *A Terre*, by Wilfred Owen

Sit on the bed. I'm blind, and three parts shell.
Be careful; can't shake hands now; never shall.
Both arms have mutinied against me – brutes.
My fingers fidget like ten idle brats.

I tried to **peg out** soldierly – no use!
One dies of war like any old disease.

A short life and a merry one my old buck!
We used to say we'd hate to live dead-old,
Yet now…I'd willingly be puffy, bald,
And patriotic. Buffers catch from boys
At least the jokes hurled at them. I suppose
Little I'd ever teach a son, but hitting,
Shooting, war, hunting, all the arts of hurting.
Well, that's what I learnt – that, and making money.

Your fifty years ahead seem none too many?
Tell me how long I've got? God! For one year
To help myself to nothing more than air!
One Spring! Is one too good to spare, too long?
Spring wind would work its way to my lung,
And grow me legs as quick as lilac shoots.

O Life, Life, let me breathe – a dug-out rat!
Not worse than ours the existences that rats lead,
Nosing along at night down some safe rut,
They find a shell-proof home before they rot.

Source J   Wilfred Owen

Remember…

- **People who fought in the First World War produced a great deal of art and poetry which tells us a lot about their experiences.**

- **These are only a few examples from the huge amount of poetry and art that was produced by people who fought in the war.**

Key words   **Peg out**   Die.

Investigations

1 Read Source **G** on page 25. How does Sassoon feel about the war? Which words in the poem tell you this?

2 Read Source **H** (page 25). How does Sassoon feel about the war in this poem? Which words in the poem tell you this?

3 Sassoon wrote both poems in Sources **G** and **H**. Which poem do you think he wrote first? Give your reasons.

4 Read Sources **I** (page 25) and **K**. Which poem do you think agrees with the view of war expressed by Otto Dix in his painting (Source **B**, page 23). Explain your choice.

5 We do not know the author of the poem in Source **I**, whereas we do know about Owen and Sassoon, the authors of the poems in Sources **G**, **H** and **K**. Do you think that this makes Source **I** less valuable as evidence about how ordinary soldiers felt about the war? Explain your answer.

6 Look back at the unit on 'Life in the trenches' on page 20. Using that, and the material in this unit, imagine you are a soldier in the First World War. Write a letter home to a member of your family. Describe how it feels to be in a trench in the war.

4 Post-war Europe

From the Great War to the 'Great Peace'

- **How did the war affect the map of Europe?**
- **How did the war affect women?**

The 'Great War' and its consequences

The First World War was known as the 'Great War'. No one knew that just over twenty years later there would be an even more devastating world war – the Second World War. To the peoples of Europe and the United States, the Great War was 'great' because of its scale. At least eight million soldiers were killed and huge areas of France and Belgium were destroyed in the fighting. The countries involved had been forced to take drastic steps in order to fight the war. The British government, for example, forced men to enlist in the army (this is called 'conscription') and took control of important industries such as the coal mines and shipbuilding.

The role of women

Women found themselves doing jobs that they would never have dreamed of doing before the war: they drove ambulances and trams, worked as shipyard workers, and worked in munitions factories. They tackled many other jobs which, until then, only men had done.

Sources **A** and **B** show clearly how the role of women changed during the war. Source **A** is an official poster from early in the war showing women waving their men off to fight. Source **B**, a photograph taken later in the war, shows women working in a munitions factory. You can read more about how women's lives changed in Chapter 9.

Political consequences

The war had many consequences. Some, like the effect it had on women, are *social* consequences. Others, such as the creation of new countries in Europe are *political*. In the short term the war also badly affected the economies of the countries involved – especially Britain. However, Britain did

Source A A poster from the early years of the First World War

Source B A photograph taken later in the war

not face the same kind of **revolution** and street violence experienced by Germany, Russia and Italy during and after the war. Britain's **democratic** political system remained intact. After all, Britain had been on the winning side and had a stable political system to see the country through the post-war crisis.

Investigations

1 Why do you think the Government made posters like Source **A**?

2 How does Source **A** show women in a traditional role?

3 How does Source **B** show the role of women in a different way?

4 Can you suggest why more and more women did jobs like the one in the munitions factory instead of what they're doing in Source **A**? (Clue: Think about the five million men who served in the army.)

Key words

Revolution A sudden and often violent change in the government of a country.

Democratic A democratic political system is one in which the people choose the government they want.

27

Fascism

Fascism started in Italy as a direct result of the problems the First World War had created in that country. Over half a million Italians were killed in a war which Italy could not afford and which did not give them the land they believed they had been promised. Although Italy had been on the winning side, Italians felt they had been treated more like a defeated country. Their reward seemed to be unemployment and poverty.

Italian workers occupied their factories and peasants seized the land from landowners. Mussolini, the leader of the **Fascists**, promised the wealthy land and factory owners that he would put a stop to all this and so they gave him their support. In 1922 Mussolini was made Prime Minister after threatening to seize power by force.

Source B
An Italian propaganda picture glorifying Mussolini

Remember...

- The war left many countries unstable and more difficult to govern, and led to violence and revolution.

- Many people, in countries like Russia and Italy, faced unemployment and poverty after the war.

- Hardship caused by the war made people angry, and ready to support new political ideas like Communism and Fascism.

Key words

Fascists People who are against the idea of democratic government and instead believe in government by one leader. Fascists want their country to have powerful armed forces to attack weaker countries.

Investigations

1 In which countries did
   a) the Communists
   b) the Fascists
   first come to power?

2 Can you suggest any difference in the way these two political groups first came to power in their countries?

3 Look at this table, which compares the beliefs of Communists and Fascists.
   Use this table and the information in this chapter to answer the following question:
   'In what ways were the views of the Communists and Fascists similar, and in what ways were they different to each other?'

Communists	Fascists
Workers should take the factories from the wealthy factory owners	The factory owners should keep their factories
Peasants should take the land from the landowners	The landowners should keep their land
Workers and peasants should be the most important groups in the country	Factory owners and landowners should be the most important groups in the country
All parties should be banned except the Communist Party	All parties should be banned except the Fascist Party
The Communist government should control all the newspapers, radio and films	The Fascist government should control all the newspapers, radio and films

Changing attitudes and declining prosperity

● *Why did some soldiers support revolution after the war?*
● *How was the British economy affected by the war?*

Revolution

Revolutions happen in a country when enough people become so angry they overthrow the existing government. After the Great War many ex-soldiers had no jobs, faced hardship and felt they had fought a war for nothing. They felt they had nothing to lose by supporting a revolution.

An important part of this change of attitude was a reaction against the existing authority – whether it was the king or the elected government.

In Sources **A**, **B** and **C**, British soldiers tell an historian their views on the war they had fought many years earlier.

Source A   Private A.J. Hooper

T owards the end of the war, we were so fed up we wouldn't even sing 'God save the King' on church parade. Never mind the bloody King, we used to say, he was safe enough; it should have been God save us.

Quoted in *The First Day of the Somme*, **by M. Middlebrook, Penguin, 1971**

Source B
Corporal
L. Jessop

M ore than anything I hated to see war-crippled men standing in the gutter selling matches. We had been promised a land fit for heroes; it took a hero to live in it. I'd never fight for my country again.

Quoted in *The First Day of the Somme*

B y the end of 1917 we couldn't care less who won as long as we could get the war over.

Quoted in *The First Day of the Somme*

Source C   Private F.W. Turner

Source D
Many soldiers returned from the war to face unemployment, as shown here in Germany in 1930

Investigations

1   What is the attitude to 'King and Country' of the soldiers in these sources?

2   Why do you think many soldiers like these, on both sides, turned against the war? (Clue: Think about battles like the Somme in Chapter 3.)

3   Which one of the men in these sources do you think would have been most likely to support a revolution in his country? Give the reasons for your answer.

4   None of the three men quoted in these sources was an officer. Does this mean the sources are less useful to an historian wanting to find out about soldiers' attitudes to the war? If so, why?

5   Why do you think a country like Italy had a revolution after the war and not Britain? (You will find some helpful information on pages 27 and 30.)

The effect of the war on Britain's economy

In 1914 Britain was a great world power – only the United States was more powerful. Britain's wealth depended on her ability to manufacture (make) goods and then sell them to other countries. The statistics in Source **F** show the economic position of the world's most powerful countries in the decades up to and after the First World War. The countries to which Britain had sold goods before the war had to find those goods from somewhere else.

This would not have mattered too much if they had gone back to buying British goods once the war was over – but they didn't. They either stuck with their new suppliers (those countries not involved in the war) or started making the goods themselves. Fewer British goods were now being sold and so workers lost their jobs and unemployment was high throughout the 1920s, even before **The Great Depression** set in during the early 1930s.

Before the war, Britain exported her goods and raw materials to many countries.

After the war, less coal, iron and steel were needed in Britain. So Britain needed to export her goods and materials again. But many countries who had bought from Britain before the war had now found new suppliers, or began to produce the goods themselves.

In 1913, Britain exported 7 million yards of cotton cloth.

During the war Britain had to produce ships, weapons and supplies. So huge quantities of coal, iron and steel were needed. This made the economy strong. Exports became less important.

In 1920, Britain exported only 4 million yards of cotton cloth.

Source E How the war affected Britain's economy

Source F The percentage share of total world manufacturing output 1880–1938. ('Manufacturing output' means goods made in factories by machines. Britain, for example, produced 23 per cent of all machine-made goods in the world in 1880. A country with a high percentage of the world's manufacturing output, such as Britain in 1880, is rich and has a strong economy.)

	1880	1900	1913	1928	1938
Britain	23	18	14	10	11
United States	15	24	32	39	31
Germany	8	13	15	12	13
France	8	7	6	6	4
Russia	8	9	8	5	9

Key words

The Great Depression A depression occurs when there is high unemployment and very little business activity. The Great Depression began in 1929 and lasted through the early 1930s.

Remember...

- **Many soldiers throughout Europe returned from the war to face unemployment and hardship.**

- **Men and women were less willing to accept old attitudes after the First World War.**

- **Britain's decline began before the First World War and continued after the war ended. The war was not, therefore, the only cause of Britain's decline, but it did make it worse.**

Investigations

'Britain was doing very well until the First World War caused the British economy to decline.' Do the statistics in Source **F** support this statement? Give reasons for your answer.

5 Depth Study: National Socialist Germany

Weimar Germany and the Nazi take-over

Why did the Germans vote for Adolf Hitler?

How did the Nazi Party come to power?

In the last chapter you read how Germany, Italy and Russia went through dramatic changes during and after the First World War. Italy and Germany faced very similar economic and political problems and in both countries **dictators** came to power. Germany's democratic system lasted until 1933 but then Adolf Hitler and his National Socialist (or Nazi) Party took over and democracy ended. There were no more elections. Opposition parties and anti-Nazi newspapers were no longer allowed.

Germans, it should be remembered, *voted* Hitler into power. The German **President**, Hindenburg, appointed Hitler as **Chancellor** in January 1933 and 17 million Germans voted for Hitler's National Socialist Party in the March 1933 elections. This came to 44 per cent of the votes. Why were so many Germans prepared to vote for a man who made no secret of his hatred for democracy, elections, free speech, and the Jews?

One reason will be clear from the last chapter. Many Germans were bitter about Germany's defeat in the First World War and the humiliating Treaty of Versailles which followed. They blamed Germany's new democratic government, the Weimar Republic, for the defeat, and for the treaty.

However, this on its own is not enough to explain Hitler's rise to power. To do this, we need to look more closely at the events of 1929–33.

Source A Number of German workers unemployed between 1924 and 1933, and as a percentage of the total workforce

Year	Number of workers unemployed	% of total workforce unemployed
1924	900 000	5
1925	700 000	3
1926	2 000 000	10
1927	1 300 000	6
1928	1 400 000	6
1929	1 900 000	8.5
1930	3 100 000	14
1931	4 500 000	22
1932	5 600 000	30
1933	3 700 000	18

Source B Number of Germans voting for the Nazi Party in elections between 1928 and 1932

Year	Germans voting for the Nazi Party
1928	800 000
1930	6 400 000
1932: July	13 700 000
Nov	11 700 000

Economic problems

Economic problems always create difficulties for a government. High unemployment levels, poor living standards and business **bankruptcies** lead many people to turn against the government in power. The crisis of 1929–33 was a very severe one, as the statistics in Source **A** show.

Investigations

1 How many German workers were unemployed in 1928? Was this a high figure? (Look at the figures for later years.) Explain your answer.

2 Why is it useful to quote the percentage of the workforce who were unemployed as well as the actual number of workers without jobs?

3 What evidence can you find in Sources **A** and **B** to support the theory that as unemployment increased, so did support for Hitler?

4 **a)** What change can you see in the number of Germans voting for the Nazi Party between July and November 1932?
   b) What reason can you find for this? (Clue: Look at the unemployment figures for 1932 and 1933.)

Key words

Dictator A person who has complete power to rule a country.
President The elected head of a republic.
Chancellor The German equivalent of a Prime Minister.
Bankruptcy A business goes bankrupt when it loses money, goes out of business and shuts down.

33

Historians believe that there was a link between the economic problems Germans faced from 1929 to 1933 and their support for the Nazi Party. Workers who had lost their jobs, shopkeepers and businessmen whose businesses had collapsed, became desperate and angry enough to vote for a man like Hitler, who promised to bring back jobs and prosperity, and they didn't care how he did it.

Political problems

If there had been a strong government in Germany between 1929 and 1933 then democracy might have survived, but the parties which made up the Weimar government were weak and could not agree over how to tackle the economic crisis. One political party after another tried to find a way out of the crisis. However, Hitler and his Nazi Party promised simple solutions and came across as united and sure of themselves.

Source C Albert Speer became Hitler's architect and later Minister for Armaments. In this extract from his memoirs Speer describes why he and his mother joined the Nazi party.

The crucial fact appeared to me to be that I personally had to choose between a future Communist Germany or a future National Socialist Germany...It must have been during these months that my mother saw an SA [*Nazi storm-troopers*] parade in the streets of Heidelberg. The sight of discipline in a time of chaos...seems to have won her over also. At any rate, without ever having heard a speech or read a pamphlet, she joined the [*Nazi*] party'.

From *Inside the Third Reich*, by Albert Speer, Weidenfeld, 1970

Source D Nazi election poster. The German slogan reads 'Our last Hope – Hitler'.

Source E This 1933 Nazi poster shows the National Socialist 'building blocks' of Work, Peace and Bread on the left, compared to the destructive plans of the Jews, Socialists and Communists on the right

This political chaos was made worse by street battles between Nazis and Communists and many wealthy Germans were afraid that Germany was on the verge of a Communist revolution, like the one in Russia. German businessmen feared that, if this took place, the Communists would take their wealth and businesses from them. Hitler promised he would crush this Communist 'threat'.

Investigations

1 Why do you think Speer's mother joined the Nazi Party?

2 To which class of people do you think the Nazis were trying to appeal in Source **D**? Give reasons for your answer.

3 Why do you think Source **E** would have persuaded Germans to vote for the Nazis?

4 Which of the two election posters do you think would have appealed most to Albert Speer? Explain your answer.

Hitler as Chancellor

In January 1933 the political situation had become so desperate that President Hindenburg decided to appoint Hitler as Chancellor. Hitler's Nazi Party was the largest in the **Reichstag** and so he was the obvious choice to lead a new government. Many influential and wealthy Germans backed Hitler – perhaps reluctantly – because they thought Hitler's 'firm' government would crush the Communists and then Hitler and his party could be replaced once the economic and political crisis was over.

In many ways Hitler was a man of his word. He said he detested democracy, Communists and Jews, and he promised jobs to the unemployed. Within two years of coming to power he had found jobs for two and a half million Germans. He destroyed democracy in Germany within six months of becoming Chancellor. He crushed the Communists and began his persecution of the Jews. Homosexuals, the disabled, and the mentally ill were also added to the Nazis' list of 'inferior stock'.

Those Germans who were not Jews, Communists, Socialists, homosexual, disabled, mentally ill or devout Christians probably thought the destruction of Germany's democratic system of government was a fair price to pay for the prosperity Hitler brought.

Hitler's dictatorship established

The first thing Hitler did as Chancellor was to call for an election in March 1933. He hoped the Nazis would get more than 50 per cent of the votes. Even though the Communists were banned from taking part in the election, the Nazis only managed to win 44 per cent of the votes. However, Hitler persuaded the Reichstag to pass the Enabling Bill. This allowed him to pass any law he wanted for four years *without* consulting Parliament. In other words, he had legally been given the power of a dictator. Hitler claimed he needed these special powers to deal with the economic crisis and the threat of a Communist revolution.

The political parties had behaved like a flock of sheep who invite the wolf into their pen. Within four months of the passing of the Enabling Bill in March, all political parties except the National Socialists had been banned and all anti-Nazi newspapers had been closed down. There were no more trade unions and no right to strike. Hitler and the Nazis had total power.

Source F The Nazis blamed the Communists for the fire which destroyed the Reichstag. This enabled Hitler to ban the Communist party.

Source G Nazi storm-troopers (SA) in 1933

Key words

Reichstag The German parliament.

Source H Nazis burning books

Remember...

- The economic crisis after 1929 brought Hitler to power.

- He promised jobs to the unemployed and he told the rich he would stamp out Communism and provide a stable government.

- He made Germans feel proud to be German after the humiliation of the Treaty of Versailles.

Investigations

1 Study Sources **G** (page 35) and **H**. Source **G** shows Hitler's storm-troopers, the SA, in 1933, the year of the Enabling Bill. Source **H** shows Nazis burning books of which they disapproved. Why are both these incidents features of a dictatorship?

2 No elections were allowed in Hitler's Germany. Even if there had been, there would not have been much point to them. Can you think why?

3 Why do you think the SA were so important to Hitler?

4 Copy out the diagram below across a full page of your exercise book or sheet of paper. Six boxes have been left empty. The statements which fit into these boxes are written below. Your task is to copy the correct statements into the right boxes on your diagram. For example, A: 'Government parties quarrelled over how

to deal the Depression' is a political problem, so it fits into the empty box on the right under the box headed 'Political crisis of 1929–33'.
A: 'Government parties quarrelled over how to deal with the Depression'.
B: 'Up to 30% of Germans had no job'.
C: 'The Treaty of Versailles made many Germans angry and bitter'.
D: 'Businessmen lost their income as firms went out of business'.
E: 'There was chaos and violence as Communists and Nazis battled in the streets'.
F: 'Hitler became Chancellor in 1933'.
Can you think of any other reason which led some Germans – especially rich ones – to support Hitler?

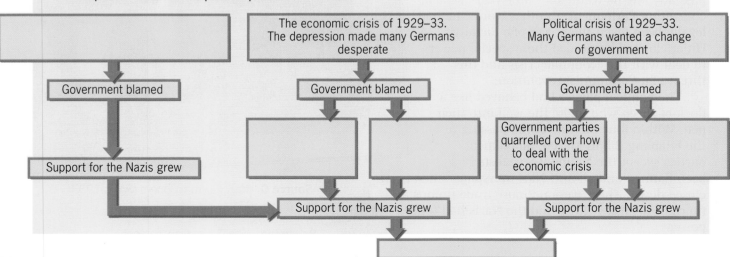

36

The Nazis in power

- **What methods did Hitler use to keep control in Germany?**
- **What was it like for women in Hitler's Germany?**
- **How is democracy different from dictatorship?**

Source A How Hitler kept control in Germany

✦ The Nazis controlled what people could read. Books and newspapers could only express or support Nazi ideas. Those which did not were burnt, or not allowed to be published.

✦ In 1934 Hitler had over 100 leaders of the SA murdered. This meant that the army and wealthy businessmen could now support the Nazis without being threatened. The support of the army was vital for Hitler's plans for war.

✦ Communists, Socialists and democrats were arrested by the Gestapo and sentenced by Nazi judges without a jury.

✦ Young people in Germany were encouraged to join Nazi youth organisations. There they were taught what to believe and how to be 'good' Nazis.

✦ On 'Crystal Night' in 1938 thousands of Jewish shops were attacked by the SA on Hitler's orders. Many Jews were arrested, and many others fled abroad.

Repression

Hitler was able to keep complete control in Germany. His first powerful way of doing this was his use of **political repression** against any possible enemies or opposition. The penalty for expressing anti-Nazi opinions was arrest by the secret police, or Gestapo, and imprisonment or execution. Suspects were always convicted because the judges were chosen by the Nazi Party because they supported Hitler. Newspapers and the radio could only publish or broadcast pro-Nazi views.

Influencing the young

The Nazis also used the more subtle methods of 'social control' by trying to influence what Germans thought. Hitler was especially keen to win the support of Germany's youth – both boys and girls – because they represented the future of Germany. Schools were strictly controlled. Only Nazi ideas and views could be taught and all teachers had to be members of the National Socialist Teachers' League.

Biology lessons were used to show how 'inferior' peoples like Jews, Blacks and Slavs (East Europeans) belonged to uncivilised races, inferior to the German race.

German youngsters were encouraged to join Nazi youth organisations like the Young Folk for 10–14 year-old boys and the Young Maidens for 10–14 year-old girls. They had smart uniforms and spent time away from their parents in camps and on mountain treks.

Prosperity

Prosperity was also very important in winning support for Hitler. If the German economy was strong and Germans were prosperous, then they would have every reason to be grateful to Hitler. If workers had jobs, a regular wage, and cheap housing, they would forget about the banning of the unions and the right to strike. Businessmen would be grateful because the workers could no longer strike or demand big wage increases and so damage business profits. Economic success was therefore an important factor in keeping Hitler in power.

On that day some 150 [SA] leaders were arrested and...executed. SS execution squads were kept busy throughout the three days of the weekend. Roehm refused to commit suicide and was executed by two SS men...Ernst of Berlin was taken off a boat at Bremen before he had time to leave for his honeymoon and was executed in Berlin semi-conscious and with a *Heil Hitler* ['Hail Hitler'] on his lips.

From *An Illustrated History of the Third Reich*, by J. Bradley, 1978

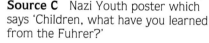

Source B An historian's account of 'The Night of the Long Knives'

The SA

Some Nazis belonged to the branch of the party called the SA (storm-troopers). They were also known as the 'Brownshirts' because of the uniform they wore. Their leader was Ernst Roehm. Roehm wanted Hitler to carry out 'socialist' policies against the rich in Germany and he also wanted the SA to replace the professional army as Germany's main military force. Hitler could not afford to lose the support of rich businessmen or the army generals. Source **B** describes his solution to the problem – 'The Night of the Long Knives' of 30 June 1934. The SS were Hitler's own 'personal protection squad'. They were keen to get rid of the leaders of their rivals, the SA, in the Nazi Party.

Source C Nazi Youth poster which says 'Children, what have you learned from the Fuhrer?'

Source D
Number of Germans out of work, 1932–38

Year	Number out of work
1932	5 600 000
1933	3 700 000
1934	2 300 000
1935	2 100 000
1936	1 600 000
1937	900 000
1938	200 000

The role of women in Hitler's Germany

Hitler was keen to see women carry out their traditional role of looking after children and the home. They were encouraged to do this from an early age. Girls aged 14 to 18 could join the League of German Maidens (BdM) and boys joined the Hitler Youth. The girls in the BdM were secretly encouraged to develop very friendly relations with the Hitler Youth so that the girls could 'donate a child to the Fuhrer', and therefore ensure that the German race remained 'racially pure'.

As many as 100 000 Hitler Youth and BdM girls attended the Nazi rally in Nuremberg in 1936 and 900 of the girls returned home pregnant. Because of this, the girls in the League got a 'bad' reputation.

Girls were directed into studying either languages or domestic science in secondary school. The school leaving certificate for domestic science pupils was nick-named 'the Pudding Level'.

Girls were discouraged from working, perming their hair, wearing make-up or trousers, smoking in public, and dieting. Smoking and slimness were thought to harm a woman's chances of bearing children. However, it should be said that many women supported these new rules.

Source E Nazi youth poster saying 'The German student fights for the Fuhrer and the People'.

Investigations

1 Sources **B** to **E** are examples of the following methods Hitler used to stay in power: **political repression**; **social control**; **economic success**. Look at all four sources and say which source belongs to which category. For example, Source **E** shows how the Nazis persuaded German youth to support their views by influencing young people's ideas. This is an example of **social control**.

2 **a)** Look at Source **D**. What happened to unemployment in Germany after 1932?
 b) Why would Hitler expect to get more support because of this?

3 What is there in Source **B** to suggest that some of the SA were loyal to Hitler?

4 Why do you think the Nazis were so keen to appeal to young people in Germany?

Source F
The Nazis encouraged large families and paid bonuses to women who had children. This Nazi poster reads 'Support the Campaign, Mother and Child.'

✦ How is democracy different from dictatorship?

• In a democracy elections are held every few years. There are a number of different parties with different ideas on how the country should be run.

• Newspapers, radio and television are free to criticise the government and all political parties.

• The government cannot control the courts or have people sent to prison simply because they don't like their opinions.

• People are free to follow whichever religious faith they choose.

• In the 1930s Britain was a democracy. Germany – between 1933 and 1945 – was not.

Investigations

1 In what ways does Source **F** fit in with the role Nazis wanted women to play?

2 How do you think German women at the time would have reacted to this poster? Explain your answer.

3 In the list of statements opposite some describe a democratic system, like that in Britain, and others describe a dictatorship.
   a) Divide your page into two columns – one headed 'Democracy' and the other 'Dictatorship', as shown here

Democracy	Dictatorship
• The government can't imprison people just because it doesn't like their views.	

b) Write each of the statements from the list in the correct column. One has been done for you. 'The government can't imprison people just because it doesn't like their views' is what happens in a democracy, so it goes in the 'Democracy' column.
c) Look at the column for 'Dictatorship'. Put a tick beside each point which you think applies to Hitler's Germany.
d) Using the information from part c), write a few sentences to answer the question 'Was Germany a dictatorship?'.

• 'Only one political party is allowed.'
• 'The law courts and police do what the government tells them.'
• 'Newspapers are allowed to criticise the government.'
• 'Elections take place every few years.'
• 'Trade unions and strikes are allowed.'
• 'Anti-government newspapers are banned.'
• 'People can be imprisoned if they speak against the government.'
• 'People are free to follow whichever religion they chose.'
• 'Trade unions and strikes are banned.'
• 'There are several political parties.'

Remember...

• **Most Germans were happy with Hitler's rule. He provided jobs and stable government.**

• **Germany had become a great country in Europe once again and its armed forces were powerful.**

• **The few who opposed Hitler were too terrified to do anything against him.**

• **The Nazis encouraged girls to carry out traditional female roles of housewife and mother.**

6 Britain and America between the wars

Prosperity and poverty

A consumer boom

In the 1920s the USA was the richest country in the world. By 1929 it was producing about 45 per cent of the world's **industrial goods**. Large numbers of Americans were able to enjoy a higher standard of living than that in other countries. By 1930, 20 million American homes had electricity, more than in the whole of the rest of the world. With electricity came a host of machines designed to make life easier for ordinary Americans. The first electric washing machine was produced in 1909 and the first dishwasher appeared in 1918. By 1928 Americans were spending $2.4 billion a year on domestic appliances. As more were bought so the companies made bigger profits. This allowed them to reduce their prices and so bring their products within the budget of still more people.

Source A
Advertisement for Easy washing machine, 1931

Source B
Advertisement for Electrolux vacuum cleaner, 1920s

All the awkward cleaning is more easily done with *Electrolux*

Source C The fifteen millionth Ford motor car

The Fifteen Millionth *Ford*

Key words **Industrial goods** Goods produced in factories.

The Depression

- **What caused the Depression?**
- **What effect did it have on the people of Britain and America?**

The causes of the Depression in the USA

The great consumer boom of the 1920s suddenly turned into the Great Depression of the 1930s. Unemployment in the USA reached 4.3 million in 1930 and 12 million in 1932. What had happened to cause this?

The main reason was the fall in demand for consumer goods. In the 1920s many people had been buying their first car, washing machine and refrigerator. By 1929 most of the people who could afford these things already had them. There were no new markets. Most Black people and farmers could still not earn enough to buy consumer goods. American companies could not sell enough abroad because the high import duties other countries used to protect their own industries made American goods too expensive.

American companies were no longer making huge profits. They cut the wages of their workers, and when the Depression continued they made many of them unemployed. As Source **A** shows, this just made things worse. There were now even fewer people who could afford to buy consumer goods.

Many powerful Americans thought that the Depression would soon be over. The President, Herbert Hoover, told Americans that 'prosperity was just around the corner'. Henry Ford closed his factory down for a few months, believing that demand would have recovered when it reopened. In fact closing down the factory simply meant there were more people with no money.

Why did the Depression spread to Britain?

The USA was the world's major economy. The Depression in America caused a collapse in world trade. Between 1929 and 1931 Britain's exports fell by a half. British companies which relied on the export trade were forced to lay off workers. Britain

Source A The spiral of economic depression

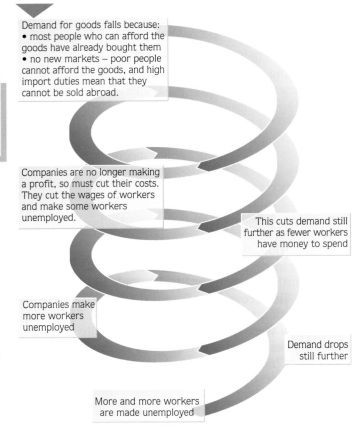

Demand for goods falls because:
- most people who can afford the goods have already bought them
- no new markets – poor people cannot afford the goods, and high import duties mean that they cannot be sold abroad.

Companies are no longer making a profit, so must cut their costs. They cut the wages of workers and make some workers unemployed.

This cuts demand still further as fewer workers have money to spend

Companies make more workers unemployed

Demand drops still further

More and more workers are made unemployed

had entered the vicious spiral of depression illustrated in Source **A**.

✦ The Wall Street Crash

On 24 October 1929 the prices of **shares** on the New York stock exchange collapsed. This became known as the Wall Street Crash. During the boom of the 1920s companies had made huge profits and so their share prices had risen. On average, share prices were five times higher in September 1929 than they had been in 1924. Buying shares seemed to be a way of making money without any risk. Even if you did not have the money to buy shares you could borrow the money from a bank or a stockbroker.

However, by 1929 there were signs that companies were not able to sell as many goods. There was a risk that with smaller profits to be made the price of shares would drop. Therefore some people decided to sell their shares. This caused share prices to fall and so other people decided to sell as well. On 24 October 13 million shares were sold and prices tumbled.

People who had bought shares on credit were in a terrible situation and many had to sell their possessions to pay back what they owed. Some had to sell their houses. Many others tried to draw their savings out of the banks, but some banks did not have the money to pay them and so were forced to close down. This meant that many people had lost their life savings.

Key words

Shares An individual's investment of money for part of the ownership of a company.

How did the Depression affect the people of Britain and America?

The Depression began in 1929 and lasted through much of the 1930s. The most immediate effect of the Depression was unemployment. Millions of people on both sides of the Atlantic lost their jobs.

In America there was no unemployment benefit and people were forced to queue for hours for free food. Many could no longer afford to pay their rent or mortgage. They had nowhere to live and had no choice but to join the 'shanty towns' that sprung up on the outskirts of many American cities. Shacks of wood and canvas were all that many Americans had to live in, as you can see in Source **B**. They came to be known as 'Hoovervilles', because President Hoover was blamed for doing so little to help these victims of the Depression.

There was 'dole' (unemployment benefit) in Britain, but with so many people unemployed the government cut the amount paid, and a hated Means Test was introduced. Families now had to declare all their money to show how poor they were. If a child got a job doing a newspaper round, then the family dole money would be cut.

Source C   In his book *The Road to Wigan Pier*, written in 1937, George Orwell describes life in the northern industrial towns in the 1930s

> I t will be seen that the income of a family on the dole normally averages around thirty shillings [£1.50] a week. One can write at least a quarter of this off as rent...A man and wife on twenty-three shillings [£1.15] a week are not far from the starvation line but they can make a home of sorts; they are vastly better off than the single man on fifteen shillings. He lives in a common lodging house, more often a furnished room, for which he usually pays six shillings a week...so he spends his days in the public library or any other place where he can keep warm.

Unemployment in England varied very much from area to area. In St. Albans, in the south-east of England, 3.9 per cent of the workforce were unemployed. In Jarrow, in the north-east, the figure was 68 per cent. In 1936 the workers of Jarrow staged a march to London to protest about unemployment and the hardship it caused.

Source D   The writer, J.B. Priestley, writing in 1934

> I had seen England. I had seen lots of Englands...There was, first, Old England, the country of cathedrals and...manor houses...But we all know this England, which at its best cannot be improved upon in this world. Then there is the industrial England of coal, iron, steel;...of thousands of rows of little houses all alike...This England makes up the larger part of the Midland and the North...but it is not being added to and has no new life poured into it.
>
> The third England is the new, post-war England...America was its real birthplace. This is the England of...giant cinemas and dance-halls,...Woolworths, motor coaches [*and*] factory girls looking like actresses...It is a cleaner, tidier, healthier, saner world than industrialism.

Remember...

- **The Depression caused terrible unemployment and poverty in both Britain and America.**
- **The boom of the 1920s was partly the cause of the Depression. By 1929 more goods were being produced than could be sold.**

Investigations

1   What does England seem like in Source **D**?

3   Can you find any evidence in the text to support this?

3   How can you explain the differences between Sources **C** and **D**?

4   Look at Sources **B** and **D**. What indications do they give that not everyone was suffering during the Depression?

45

Government action

- What did the British and American governments do to overcome the Depression?
- Why did they choose different policies?
- How successful were these policies?

Roosevelt and the New Deal

In November 1932 the USA elected a new president, Franklin D. Roosevelt. He promised to put an end to the Depression and help the unemployed. He said the government would spend money to create jobs and make workers better off. The workers would then be able to buy more goods, and companies would begin to employ more workers. This policy was known as the 'New Deal'.

Help for the unemployed

The WPA – the Works Progress Administration – created millions of jobs building roads, schools and hospitals. The CCC – the Civilian Conservation Corps – found work for young men planting trees to prevent soil erosion and creating national parks. Roosevelt also created the Federal Emergency Relief Act so that emergency funds could be given to the unemployed until jobs were created for them. In 1935 Roosevelt also introduced unemployment benefit, though since this was run by the individual states it varied greatly across America.

Source A A contemporary American cartoon about the success of the New Deal

Help for farmers

Roosevelt also tried to help the farmers. The Agricultural Adjustment Act (AAA) paid farmers to grow less food so that prices would rise and make farming profitable again. However, not all of the money went to the farmers. In the south it was the poor sharecroppers who had to grow less cotton, but the AAA paid the money direct to their landlords. The landlords were supposed to pass this money on to the sharecroppers, but many did not. This left thousands of sharecroppers far worse off than they had been before.

The cost of the New Deal

Roosevelt's policies were very expensive. The government had to spend far more money than it earned from taxes. This is called a *budget deficit*. Many people thought that running a budget deficit would lead to **inflation** and ruin the American economy.

Key words   **Inflation**   A situation where prices rise and money is worth less.

Britain and the balanced budget

The British government disagreed with Roosevelt's solution to the Depression. They believed that the government must spend less rather than more, to *prevent* a budget deficit. That is why the British government cut the amount spent on unemployment benefit. To try and help British companies to recover, the government introduced import duties on foreign goods. They thought that British people would now buy goods produced in Britain, as they would be cheaper. However, this did not solve the problem. So many people in England were unemployed or had had their wages cut that they could not afford to buy goods, wherever they were made.

With the increasing threat of the power of Hitler's Germany, the British government also decided to build more weapons, especially aeroplanes for the Air Force. This was also done to create more jobs. In 1934 the Special Areas Act was introduced to try and encourage companies to move their factories to areas of high unemployment. However, only £2 million was given to this project and so it created few jobs.

Which government was the more successful?

The British government believed that it would be a disaster to follow Roosevelt's policies. Yet in America Roosevelt was a hero who was re-elected as President in 1936, 1940 and again in 1944. He was regarded as the man who had helped to end the Depression. Does the evidence support this view or were the British government right?

Source C   Unemployment in Britain 1929–40

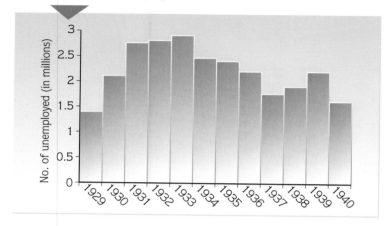

Source D   Unemployment in the USA 1932–45

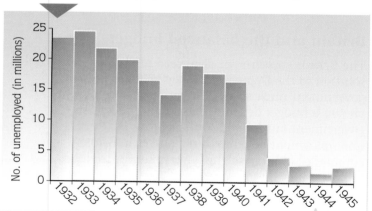

Source E   From *The Road to Wigan Pier* by George Orwell

When you see the unemployment figures [*for Great Britain*] quoted at two millions, it is fatally easy to take this as meaning that two million people are out of work and the rest of the population is comparatively comfortable…This is an enormous under-estimate, because…the only people shown on unemployment figures are those drawing the dole – that is, in general, heads of families,…a Labour Exchange [*Job Centre*] officer told me that to get at the real number of people living on the dole, you have to multiply the official figures by something over three.

Source F   New houses built in Britain by private companies 1929–37

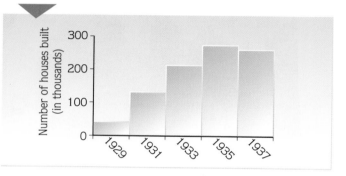

Source G   Neville Chamberlain, the Chancellor of the Exchequer, in his Budget speech of 1933

Look around the world today and you see that badly unbalanced budgets are the rule rather than the exception…I find that budget deficits repeated year after year may be accompanied by deepening recession…Of all the countries passing through these difficult times the one that has stood the test with the greatest measure of success is the United Kingdom.

Remember…

- **Both the British and American governments claimed that their policies helped to end the Depression.**
- **The American government tried to cure unemployment by borrowing money to create jobs and consumers who would buy goods and so create more jobs.**
- **Unemployment in Great Britain was higher than the official figures.**
- **Only the Second World War finally brought an end to the Depression.**

Investigations

1   Read Source **E**. In what way does it suggest that Sources **C** and **D** may be inaccurate?

2   In Source **G** Chamberlain says that Britain has been most successful in dealing with the Depression.
   a) Does Source **F** support Chamberlain's statement? Explain your answer.
   b) Does Source **C** support Chamberlain's statement? Explain your answer.
   c) Do you think that Source **C** or Source **F** is the more important in deciding whether Britain had overcome the Depression? Explain your answer.

3   Was the New Deal a success? Use Sources **A** (page 46), **B** (page 47) and **D** as well as the text to explain your answer.

7 Global war
Dictators in control

- **Why was it so easy for Hitler to get his way?**
- **What were Hitler's plans for expansion?**

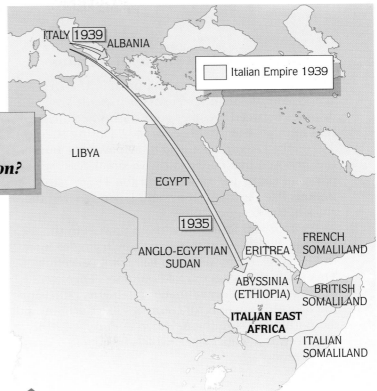

Source A Italian expansion into Abyssinia

Aggression

The war broke out in Europe in September 1939 when the German armed forces invaded Poland. Hitler and the actions of Nazi Germany clearly played a major part in causing the war but it is important to consider other factors as well. Hitler was not the only dictator in the world with aggressive plans. The actions of dictators like Mussolini and Hirohito, the **Emperor** of Japan, showed Hitler that you could get what you wanted by threatening or using force.

Italy and Japan

The Italian dictator Mussolini and Emperor Hirohito of Japan did not directly cause the Second World War. But their aggressive policies made war more likely because they showed that aggression and force could succeed. In 1931 Japan invaded Chinese Manchuria. No attempt was made to stop them. They followed this with an invasion of the rest of China in 1937. Japan managed to occupy vast areas of China while the rest of the world stood by and watched.

Mussolini, the Fascist dictator of Italy, did much the same. In 1935 Italy invaded Abyssinia (now Ethiopia) in Africa and took control of it. Later, Italian troops occupied Albania. Britain and France criticised Italy's actions but did nothing to stop them.

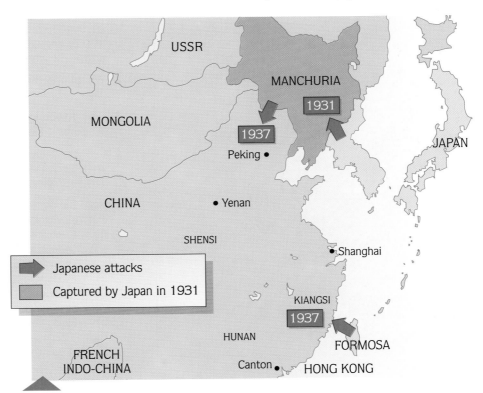

Source B Japanese invasions of Manchuria and China

Hitler watched all these events. He believed the democratic powers – Britain, France, and the USA – would not stand up to Germany. He thought he could grab what territory he wanted and nobody would stop him.

The failure of the League of Nations

The League of Nations was set up after the First World War. Its main purpose was to settle disputes between member countries peacefully so that another war could be avoided. During the 1920s the League managed to achieve this, but in this period it had only dealt with small, less powerful countries. However, in the 1930s, stronger nations like Germany, Italy, and Japan ignored the rules of the League.

Britain and France, the main powers in the League, did not want to risk war by trying to force these aggressive powers into behaving peacefully. This made the League weaker and less effective. Many times the League made statements criticising the aggressive actions of countries like Germany, but did nothing to stop them. Hitler soon realised the League was a 'paper tiger' which he could safely ignore.

Source C   Germany's plans for expansion

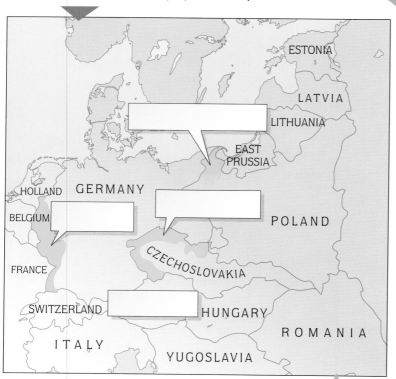

- **Hitler planned to expand Germany by seizing neighbouring states especially those where there were Germans living.**

- **The aggressive actions of Italy and Japan convinced Hitler he could do the same in Europe without opposition.**

Hitler's plans for German expansion

Hitler was determined to tear up the Treaty of Versailles (see page 28) and ignore its restrictions on Germany's military power. He wanted to take over neighbouring territories that he thought should belong to Germany:

- The Rhineland – the area between France and Germany.
- Austria – a German-speaking country on Germany's southern border.
- The Sudetenland region of Czechoslovakia, with three million Germans living there.
- The Polish Corridor – a part of Poland with three million German inhabitants, which had belonged to Germany before the First World War.

This expansion was forbidden by the Treaty of Versailles. But Hitler was convinced that Britain and France would not stand up to him, and that Czechoslovakia and Poland were too weak to stop him on their own.

Investigations

1   Britain and France both disapproved of the actions of Italy and Japan, but they were not willing to do anything to stop them. Do Sources **A** and **B** on page 49 help to explain why? (Clue: Where are the places being attacked? Where are Britain and France?)

2   What important lesson did Hitler learn from Italy and Japan?

3   Why do you think the League of Nations was so weak? Why was it like a 'paper tiger'?

4   Can you think of any reasons why Britain and France were so desperate to avoid war with Germany? (Clue: The First World War)

5   Read the paragraph 'Hitler's plans for German expansion'. Copy the map into your exercise book and fill in the blank boxes with the correct name of each area. Look at your completed map and answer the following:
    a) Why do you think France was so worried when German troops entered the Rhineland? (Clue: On whose border is the Rhineland?)
    b) Why do you think the Czechs were so worried by Hitler's occupation of Austria?
    c) Can you think why Hitler wanted to take over the Polish Corridor, apart from the fact there were Germans living there? (Clue: Look at what territories are on either side of the 'Corridor')
    d) Before Hitler invaded Poland, he made a secret agreement with another country in which that country would also invade Poland, but from the east. Which country was it? Can you think why this was rather surprising? (Clue: Think about Hitler's views on Communism)

Remember...

The road to war

The Rhineland and Austria

In March 1936 Hitler sent German troops into the Rhineland. France was ready to use force against Germany but only if Britain supported her. Britain refused and the German troops stayed. Hitler was even more convinced of the feebleness of Britain and France and so his next move was still bolder. In March 1938 German troops occupied Austria and united it with Germany. This was another illegal move but there was little protest from Britain and France.

The Sudetenland and the Munich Crisis

Six months later Hitler demanded the Sudetenland, which had become part of Czechoslovakia after the break up of the old Austro-Hungarian Empire at the end of the First World War. Three million Germans lived there. Hitler promised this would be his last demand for territory. The Czechs were furious and ready to fight to keep their land. But Chamberlain, the British Prime Minister, and Daladier, the French Prime Minister, made it clear that their countries would not help the Czechs if they went to war with Germany. An agreement was signed in Munich in September 1938 and the Sudetenland became German.

The invasion of Poland

In March 1939, German troops seized the rest of Czechoslovakia. At last Chamberlain and Daladier realised that Hitler could not be trusted. The following month they promised Poland that if the Germans attacked them, Britain and France would declare war on Germany. Hitler did not believe that they would keep this promise (and who could blame him?) so he invaded Poland on 1 September 1939. To his surprise, both France and Britain declared war on Germany two days later. The war in Europe had begun.

Source A German troops marching into the Rhineland in March 1936

Was Chamberlain right or wrong?

Looking back over the events which led up to the outbreak of war in 1939, it is easy to see that Chamberlain was mistaken to go on believing Hitler's promises that he would not demand any more territory. It is clear that Hitler wanted to dominate Europe and was ready to use force to do so. If Chamberlain (or Stanley Baldwin, the Prime Minister before him) had stood up to Hitler, then war might have been avoided. Sources **B–F** on page 52 look at certain aspects of Britain in the 1930s and provide evidence to help explain why Chamberlain did nothing to stop Hitler in the years up to 1939.

Mass Observation was an organisation whose task was to interview ordinary people in Britain at the time to get their views on current events. In September 1938 they interviewed people on what they felt about Chamberlain's agreement with Hitler at Munich concerning the Sudetenland. Sources **E** and **F** (page 52) give two very different responses from this survey.

Source B Chamberlain made this speech about the First World War at a meeting in July 1938

W hen I think of those four terrible years and I think of the seven million young men who died, the thirteen million who were maimed and mutilated, then I have to say: in war there are no winners, but all are losers. It is those thoughts which have made me feel that it was my duty to avoid another Great War in Europe.

Source C Crowds in Downing Street cheering Chamberlain (top window, centre) after his return from the meeting with Hitler in Munich, September 1938

Source D Numbers of aircraft built by France, Britain and Germany, 1933–39

	1933	1934	1935	1936	1937	1938	1939
France	600	600	785	890	743	1382	3163
Britain	633	740	1140	1877	2123	2827	7940
Germany	368	1968	3183	5112	5606	5235	8295

Source E From a Mass Observation interview of a man aged 70

I think Chamberlain's doing wrong…Why shouldn't the Czechs fight for their country? Why should we allow a bully like Hitler to dominate Europe? Let's fight him and finish it.

Source F From one woman's Mass Observation interview

I have been collecting poisons for some time…I have sufficient to give myself, husband and all the children a lethal dose. I can remember the last war. I don't want to live through another, or the children either. I shan't tell them. I shall just do it.

Remember…

- **Hitler got his way in Europe because Britain and France were desperate to avoid another war.**

Investigations

1 Read through the text again and complete the Timeline below. Fill in the events which took place at these times:

Date	Event
March 1936	
March 1938	
September 1938	
March 1939	
April 1939	
1 September 1939	
3 September 1939	

2 Which 'four terrible years' was Chamberlain referring to in Source **B**?

3 Does Source **D** suggest why Britain and France did well to avoid war with Germany until 1939? Explain your answer.

4 Do you think the woman in Source **F** would have agreed more with Chamberlain or the man in Source **E**? Give reasons for your answer.

5 What do Sources **C**, **E** and **F** suggest about public opinion on Chamberlain's actions at Munich?

6 'These sources prove that Chamberlain was right to avoid war with Hitler until 1939'. Do you agree? Give reasons for your answer.

Global war: Triumph of the Axis Powers, 1939–42

Global war

The war which started with the invasion of Poland eventually spread beyond Europe into North Africa and then the Far East. It was fought in the skies and at sea. Each country involved had to get its entire population to contribute to the war. Civilians were targeted by bombers and went hungry as rationing was introduced, though not in the United States. The war took over every aspect of people's lives. It was a total war in which 50 million people died.

The Axis Powers

The war can be roughly divided into two halves. The first half from 1939 to mid-1942 saw a run of victories by the so-called 'Axis' powers: Germany, Japan and Italy. The Allied powers – Britain, Russia and the United States – were mostly on the defensive. During 1942 the Axis Powers weakened and the Allies gradually turned the tables and began a series of decisive victories which ended with the defeat of Italy in September 1943, Germany in May 1945, and finally Japan in August 1945.

The battle for Britain

Poland surrendered quickly in early October 1939 after a series of rapid tank attacks and bombing from aircraft. For the next six months there was no fighting on land. This period of quiet was known as the 'Phoney War' but it was ended suddenly with the German invasion of Norway in April 1940 and then France a month later. France lasted only six weeks before surrendering to Germany and Italy. Mussolini had entered the war on Germany's side in June 1940 when he was sure Britain was beaten.

Mussolini was wrong. Hitler planned to invade Britain but failed to gain control of the skies in the summer of 1940. The RAF defeated the German air force in the Battle of Britain and the invasion was called off. Britain was saved because Hitler's attention was somewhere else.

'Operation Barbarossa'

In June 1941 Hitler launched a huge invasion army of 3 million men and 3 500 tanks against Communist Russia in what was known as Operation Barbarossa. The Russians, taken by surprise, were pushed backwards as city after city fell to the powerful German tank columns. By the end of 1941 three million Russian soldiers had been taken prisoner by the Germans. Moscow and victory now seemed within easy reach.

Source A 'Operation Barbarossa'– the German invasion of Russia, June 1941

Reasons for the early success of the Axis Powers

There are several possible explanations for the early successes of the German and Japanese forces. Sometimes one side wins because it has more powerful armed forces or industrial resources. Sometimes the successful side uses a new strategy which takes the other by surprise. Study Sources **B** to **E** to decide which of the above reasons might explain the early victories of the Axis Powers.

Source C Military aircraft production for 1941 (numbers of fighters and bombers). Planes were the single most important weapon of the war. Whoever controlled the skies would win the war.

Allies		Axis Powers	
Britain	11 700	Germany	7 100
Russia	10 800	Italy	2 100

Source E Steel production for 1941 (in millions of tonnes). Steel is a vital industrial resource for a country at war. It is needed to make ships, tanks, planes, shells, and guns.

Allies		Axis Powers	
Britain	12	Germany	28
Russia	18	Italy	2
Canada	2		

Source B Oil production for 1941 (in millions of tonnes). Oil was the single most important industrial resource of the war. Without oil, planes, tanks, ships, and transport could not function.

Allies		Axis Powers	
Britain	14	Germany	6
Russia	33	Romania	5.5
Canada	1	Italy	0.1

Source D New ways of fighting a war can often bring quick victories – until the enemy finds a way of dealing with them or even copies them. The Germans developed a new style of war called 'Blitzkrieg'. Here is a dictionary definition of what this word means.

> A term [*literally 'lightning war'*]...to describe the German armed forces use of fast-moving tanks and deep-ranging aircraft...Blitzkrieg tactics were used with great success by the Germans in 1939–1941 to achieve rapid and conclusive [*decisive*] victories.
>
> **From Chambers *Dictionary of World History*, 1993**

Remember...

- **The Germans were successful at first because they used new and daring tactics – the Blitzkrieg – and because they had the advantage of surprise.**

- **The Germans were successful not because they had more or better military equipment, but because they simply used them more effectively.**

Investigations

1 Which side produced most oil in 1941 – Allies or Axis?

2 Which side built the greatest numbers of aircraft in 1941?

3 Does Source **E** suggest that the Axis Powers lost the war because they could not produce enough steel? Explain your answer.

4 Can you think of any countries invaded by Germany where the Blitzkrieg was used?

5 Why was Blitzkrieg not successful against Britain? (Clue: Think about Britain's geographical position)

6 Do Sources **B** and **C** suggest any reason why Germany eventually lost the war? Use the sources to support your answer.

1942: The year of three turning-points

Midway: Pacific turning-point

Up to now, the USA had remained neutral in the war. However, on 7 December 1941 Japan launched a surprise attack against the US Pacific naval fleet in its base at Pearl Harbor in Hawaii, and against British and American bases elsewhere in the Far East. The USA was now at war with Japan. Four days after the attack on Pearl Harbor, Germany and Italy also declared war on the United States in support of their Japanese ally. The war was now truly global.

The Japanese won victory after victory for the next six months until the US fleet won a victory over the Japanese navy at the Battle of Midway in June 1942. From now on, the US forces were on the advance against Japan and the Japanese began to retreat.

El Alamein: North African turning-point

Italian troops invaded British-controlled Egypt but made little progress even though the British forces were heavily outnumbered by the Italians. Only when Hitler sent troops to help his Italian allies in 1941 did the Axis forces make real advances against the British, Australian and New Zealand troops. However, in November 1942 the run of Axis victories in the desert came to a end at the battle of El Alamein. This battle saved the Suez Canal and the Middle East oil fields from capture by the German–Italian forces and was one of three major turning-points in that year. It meant that Germany would continue to be short of precious fuel for her tanks and trucks fighting in the desert.

Source A This photograph shows that the Russian troops were well-prepared to fight in the freezing weather conditions, unlike the German forces

Stalingrad: Russian turning-point

The string of German victories in Russia came to an end at the Battle of Stalingrad (November 1942 – January 1943). Had the Germans won this battle they might have captured the vast Russian oil supplies in the Caucasus. A German army of 330 000 men was killed or captured. It was Germany's biggest defeat of the war so far and proved that the Germans could be beaten. Now it was turn of the Russians to go on the attack.

Hitler expected his invasion of Russia to be over before the winter of 1941, so his troops were not supplied with winter clothing or equipped for low temperatures. Many froze to death. The Russians, on the other hand, were well-prepared for the cold Russian winter, as Source **A** shows.

Investigations

1 What were the three turning-point battles of 1942?

2 **a)** What did the battles of Stalingrad and El Alamein have in common? (Clue: A vital raw material)
b) How would Germany have benefited if they had won either or both of the battles of El Alamein and Stalingrad?

Key words

Turning-point An event which causes a major change.

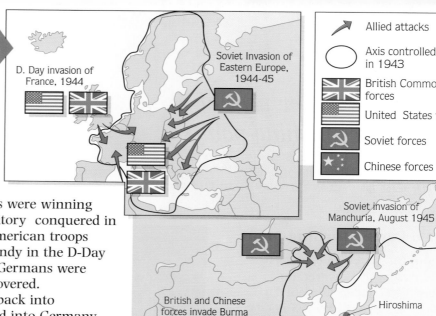

Source B
The defeat of the Axis Powers

Allied victory

The Italians surrendered to the Allies in September 1943 after overthrowing their dictator, Mussolini. Russian forces drove the German army back out of Russia. In the Pacific, British and US forces were winning back from the Japanese the territory conquered in 1942. In Europe, British and American troops landed on French soil in Normandy in the D-Day Landings on 6 June 1944. The Germans were taken by surprise and never recovered.

German troops were forced back into Germany. Russian soldiers moved into Germany from the east. Hitler shot himself in April 1945 rather than be taken prisoner. Germany surrendered a few days later, in May 1945. The war in Europe was over.

The end of the war in the Pacific

In the Pacific the US troops faced an enemy who were prepared to die rather than surrender. Progress was slow against the Japanese, and American losses were high.

Oil production (in millions of tonnes)			
Allies		**Axis Powers**	
Britain	21	Germany	6
Russia	18	Romania	3.5
USA	220	Japan	1

Aircraft production (fighters and bombers)			
Allies		**Axis Powers**	
Britain	19 000	Germany	28 000
Russia	22 000	Japan	19 000
USA	74 000		

Tank production			
Allies		**Axis Powers**	
Britain	5 000	Germany	19 000
Russia	29 000	Japan	400
USA	18 000		

Steel production (in millions of tonnes)			
Allies		**Axis Powers**	
Britain	12	Germany	26
Russia	12	Japan	6.5
USA	85		

Source **B** shows how the Axis Powers had to fight on many fronts. This was a major cause of the Axis defeat.

Source C
Production of oil, aircraft, tanks and steel by the Allies and Axis Powers in 1944

After the capture of Okinawa in June 1945, the Americans could invade Japan itself, but decided that too many American lives would be lost – even though Japan had virtually no air force or navy left. Instead, President Truman ordered the dropping of atomic bombs on the Japanese cities of Hiroshima and Nagasaki in August 1945 as the quickest way to achieve victory. The bombs killed 125 000 civilians instantly and many more died within weeks. Japan surrendered a week later on 14 August. The world war was over.

The information in Source **C** helps to explain why the Germans and Japanese lost the war.

Investigations

1 The British and Americans claimed that their bombing raids badly damaged German production of steel, tanks and aircraft. Does Source **C** support this? Give reasons for your answer. (Look at the figures for 1941 in Sources **B–E** on page 54 for comparison.)

2 'The entry of the United States into the war was the most important reason for the defeat of Germany and Japan'. Explain why you agree or disagree with this statement.

Remember...

- **The Axis Powers lost because they were fighting on too many fronts.**

- **Once the US entered the war, Japan and Germany could not match the industrial power of the Allies.**

- **The Axis Powers never had enough oil.**

Depth Study: The Holocaust

- **How did the Nazis encourage anti-Semitism?**
- **What was 'the Final Solution'?**
- **Where did the Holocaust take place?**

'Whom shall I shoot first?'

Source A Rivka Yosselevska, a survivor of a Nazi mass shooting of Jews in 1942, describes her experience in 1961 to a court in Jerusalem

Source B Nazi SA troopers stand outside a Jewish shop in 1933. The placard reads 'Germans! Beware! Don't buy from Jews'.

> And then my turn came. There was my younger sister, and she wanted to leave; she pleaded with the German; she asked to run, naked; she went up to the Germans with one of her friends; they were embracing each other; and she asked to be spared, standing there naked. He looked into her eyes and shot the two of them. They fell together in their embrace, the two young girls, my sister and her young friend. Then my second sister was shot and then my turn came.
>
> We turned towards the grave and then he turned around and asked, 'Whom shall I shoot first?'. We were already facing the grave. The German asked, 'Whom do you want me to shoot first?'. I did not answer. I felt him take the child from my arms. The child cried out and was shot immediately. And then he aimed at me. First he held on to my hair and turned my head around; I stayed standing; I heard a shot, but I continued to stand and then he turned my head again and he aimed the revolver at me, ordered me to watch, and then turned my head around and shot at me. Then I fell to the ground into the pit amongst the bodies; but I felt nothing.'

Quoted in *The Holocaust* by Martin Gilbert, Collins 1986

Rivka was not dead. She later crawled her way out of the pit of the dead and dying, was hidden by a Russian farmer and survived the war. Six million other Jewish men, women and children did not. They were victims of a Nazi campaign of mass-murder called the Holocaust and the people who carried out the campaign believed in anti-semitism.

How did the Nazis encourage anti-semitism?

Anti-semitism is the hatred and persecution of Jews. Hitler did not invent it. Anti-semitism existed everywhere in Europe and had done for many centuries. Hitler went further and created a political party based on it.

To begin with, the Nazis only made life difficult for the Jews of Germany. Hitler was unsure how other Germans and other countries would react, so his anti-Jewish policies began only gradually. Non-Jews, called Aryans by Hitler, were told not to buy from Jewish shops. Jewish dentists and doctors were forbidden to treat 'Aryan' Germans, and marriage between Jew and Aryan was not allowed. Germans who continued to use Jewish shops or services had their names put up on posters under the title 'Race Traitor'.

Investigations

1 Do you think the method used in Source **B** would be successful in discouraging people from using Jewish shops? Give reasons for your answer.

2 What do you suppose the Nazis meant by calling someone a 'Race Traitor'?

3 Hitler had hated Jews long before he came to power. Why do you think he used relatively mild measures against them at first, as in Source **B**, instead of having them killed straight away?

Hitler's 'Final Solution'

It was only after the Second World War had begun that the Nazis began what they called 'the Final Solution' – the planned mass-murder of all of the Jews in territory occupied by the German army. Hitler was obsessed with his hatred of the Jews. He believed that they caused Germany's defeat in the First World War and infected the German race.

He now planned to wipe out all the Jews in Europe. There were many others in Europe who helped Hitler in this campaign of mass-murder, including Poles, Ukrainians and those French who worked with the Nazis after France was invaded by Germany in 1940.

The death camps

The Nazis calculated that there were three million Jews in Poland and another one and a quarter million in Russia. In 1942 they decided that all of Europe's eleven million Jews would perish in 'the Final Solution'. Himmler, the head of the **SS**, was given the task of organising it. At first, Jews were rounded up in their hundreds and even thousands and shot in front of huge pits like the one described at the beginning of this chapter.

This method was too slow and inefficient. Nazi Special Action Squads tried gassing Jews in air-tight vans with engine exhaust fumes, but this could take up to 30 minutes and only worked with small numbers. Himmler decided that bigger gas chambers were needed which could hold as many as 2000 and that cyanide gas would be used. This took just 15 minutes. The bodies could then be burned.

When the Jews arrived at a death camp like Auschwitz they were lined up and told to go to the right or left. Those unable to work went to the right: the elderly, mothers with small children, pregnant women, children under eleven. The rest went to the left where they were spared for a few months until they were worked to death. A few survived until the end of the war. For those not selected for work, death in the gas chambers was immediate.

Why didn't they resist? In most cases, the victims did not realise what was about to happen to them. The SS went to a lot of trouble to make sure they went to their deaths unsuspecting. They were told they were to have showers for reasons of hygiene.

Key words

SS The *Schutz Staffeln* – Hitler's own private army.

Investigations

Sources **B** and **C** both show acts of anti-semitism. In what ways are they different?

Source D A description of how Jews were prepared for the gas chambers

The voice over the loudspeaker told them to form into rows of five for 'selection'. The voice explained what that meant. The strongest would be selected for work; the old and sick would be sent to the infirmary; all others would receive showers and be taken care of....

Signs in the undressing hall read: Clean is Good, Lice Can Kill, Wash Yourself. Crude, insulting even. But, under the circumstances not out of place. Next, the women were told to turn their valuables over to the guards for safe-keeping....

Up to the last minute, the SS deceived the women with normal-sounding phrases: 'Tie both shoes well, and put your clothing in one pile, because they will be handled back to you at the end of the showers'.

From *A Nightmare in History, The Holocaust 1939–1945* by M. Chaikin, Houghton-Mifflin 1987

And what of the men who carried out these crimes? We might like to think that only the criminally insane could take a child from the arms of its mother and beat its brains out against the side of a railway wagon before calmly handing it back. Some Nazis were fanatics who enjoyed what they did, but most were 'normal' people who believed they were acting honourably in 'defending' their country in a time of war. Himmler once attended a mass shooting of Jews in Russia. An SS colonel later described Himmler's reaction.

Source E Himmler's reaction to a Nazi shooting squad

After the shooting was over, Himmler gathered the shooting squad in a semi-circle around him and, standing in his car,...he made a speech. He had seen for himself how hard the task was which they had to fulfil for Germany...But however terrible it all might be, even for him as a mere spectator, and how much worse it must be for them, the people who had to carry it out, he could not see any way round it.

From *The Holocaust* by M. Gilbert

'Don't say "Mama"'

There is a great deal of evidence to describe the horrors of these events – much of it painful to read. Sometimes the worst events do not contain horrible details of death or torture, but express the terrible anguish that was suffered.

The incident in Source **F** is described by an eye-witness. Eliezer Melamed tells how a mother hid herself and her children from German soldiers searching for Jews to send to the death camps – a fate about which some Jews, like these, eventually got to know.

Source F An eye-witness account

The mother hid in one corner of the room, the three children in another. The Germans entered the room and discovered the children. One of the children, a young boy, began to scream, 'Mama! Mama!' as the Germans dragged the children away. But another of them...shouted to his brother in Yiddish [*the language of some Jews*]...'Don't say "Mama", they'll take her too'.

The boy stopped screaming. The mother remained silent. Her children were dragged away. The mother was saved. 'I will always hear that,' Melamed recalled, 'especially at night: "Don't say "Mama". And I will always remember the sight of the mother as she watched her children being dragged away by the Germans. She was hitting her head against the wall, as if to punish herself for remaining silent, for wanting to live.

Quoted in *The Holocaust* by M. Gilbert

The boy who had saved his mother was just four years old.

Investigations

1 What methods does Source **D** show that the SS used to keep the Jews from suspecting that they were about to be gassed?

2 Does your answer to Question 1 prove that the SS wanted to ease the suffering of the Jews or can you think of another reason for their methods?

3 Does Source **E** suggest that Himmler enjoyed what the SS were doing? Use evidence from the source to explain your answer.

4 Can you explain why the fact that the SS wasn't full of crazed maniacs makes the events of the Holocaust all the more terrible?

Where did the Holocaust take place?

Look at Source **G** which shows where the victims of the Holocaust came from.

Source G The numbers of Jews from each country murdered in the Holocaust

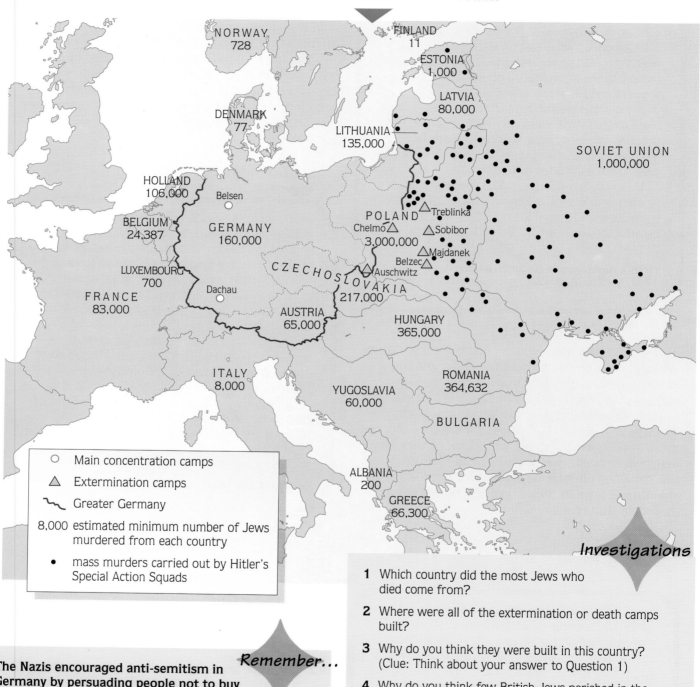

NORWAY
728

FINLAND
11

ESTONIA
1,000

DENMARK
77

LATVIA
80,000

LITHUANIA
135,000

SOVIET UNION
1,000,000

HOLLAND
106,000

Belsen

BELGIUM
24,387

GERMANY
160,000

POLAND
3,000,000

Chelmo △ Treblinka △
△ Sobibor
△ Majdanek

Belzec △
Auschwitz △

LUXEMBOURG
700

Dachau

CZECHOSLOVAKIA
217,000

FRANCE
83,000

AUSTRIA
65,000

HUNGARY
365,000

ITALY
8,000

YUGOSLAVIA
60,000

ROMANIA
364,632

BULGARIA

ALBANIA
200

GREECE
66,300

○ Main concentration camps

△ Extermination camps

〜 Greater Germany

8,000 estimated minimum number of Jews murdered from each country

● mass murders carried out by Hitler's Special Action Squads

Remember...

- **The Nazis encouraged anti-semitism in Germany by persuading people not to buy from Jewish people or use their services.**

- **'The Final Solution' was Hitler's plan for the mass-murder of all Jews in Europe.**

- **The mass-murder of Jews by the Nazis took place mainly in death camps in Poland, although mass shottings of Jews were carried out throughout Eastern Europe and in Russia.**

Investigations

1 Which country did the most Jews who died come from?

2 Where were all of the extermination or death camps built?

3 Why do you think they were built in this country? (Clue: Think about your answer to Question 1)

4 Why do you think few British Jews perished in the Holocaust? (Clue: Did the Germans occupy Britain?)

5 Hitler invaded eastern Europe because he wanted it for Germans to live in. Does this map suggest another reason?

6 Can you think why it was the Russian army, rather than the British and Americans, who first discovered what had taken place in the extermination camps?

Depth Study: The destroyer of worlds

Why did the Americans drop the atom bombs on Japan?

Source A   Dresden after the British bombing

A people's war?

Between 1936 and 1939 there was a civil war in Spain between the Fascists and the Communists. Germany supported the Spanish fascists. On 26 April 1937 German planes bombed the Spanish town of Guernica, killing 800 people and injuring thousands more. Civilians were now a major target in war. Germany continued these tactics in the Second World War. On 14 November 1940 the Germans bombed Coventry, killing another 400 civilians. Many other British cities, such as Plymouth and Bristol, became targets. President Roosevelt described these attacks as '…inhuman barbarism that has profoundly shocked the conscience of humanity'.

Yet the British and the Americans were to use these same tactics with much greater savagery. In February 1945 a British bombing raid on the German city of Dresden resulted in the deaths of at least 35 000 people. Finally, on 6 August 1945, the Americans dropped an atom bomb on the Japanese city of Hiroshima, killing at least 70 000. Why did the Allies use such 'inhuman barbarism'? This depth study provides evidence to help you decide why the Americans used the atom bomb.

The Manhattan Project

During the Second World War both the Germans and the Americans had been trying to build an atom bomb, a weapon so powerful that it would surely win the war. The British managed to slow down the Germans' work on their bomb by sabotaging their laboratories in Norway. When the Germans surrendered in May 1945 they had still not succeeded in developing a bomb. The American attempt to build an atom bomb was code named 'The Manhattan Project'. The scientists involved were based in a remote area of New Mexico in the south of the USA. In July 1945 they finally succeeded in exploding an atom bomb. It was too late to use it to defeat Germany, but Japan had still not surrendered.

6 August 1945

On 6 August a single US bomber, the Enola Gay, dropped an atom bomb, nicknamed 'Little Boy' on the Japanese city of Hiroshima. Three days later a second bomber dropped a second bomb, of a different design and known as 'Fat Man', on the city of Nagasaki. Together the two bombs killed more than 100 000 people immediately and the radiation may have killed another half a million people in the years after the war. On 14 August the Emperor of Japan ordered Japan to surrender.

August 7:   Hundreds of injured people trying to escape passed our house. The sight of them was almost unbearable. Their faces and hands were burnt and swollen, and great sheets of skin had peeled away from their tissues to hang down like rags on a scarecrow. This morning they had stopped. I found them lying on both sides of the road so thick that it was impossible to pass without stepping on them.

Source B
Diary of Dr. Tabuchi, an eye-witness of the bombing of Hiroshima

Investigations

1 Read Source **B** and then look at Source **C** on page 62. What does Source **B** tell you that is not in the photograph?

2 Do you think that Source **B** is more or less useful than Source **C** in helping to understand the effects of the bomb?

3 Is a photograph more or less reliable than a written account such as Source **B**? Explain your answer.

Source C Hiroshima after the dropping of the atom bomb

By 1945 the Americans were ready to attack the main islands of Japan, but they needed to recapture islands near to Japan as air bases for their bombers. Iwo Jima and Okinawa were chosen as the targets. Iwo Jima was a small island defended by 25 000 Japanese troops. It took four months to capture and the Japanese fought to the death. There were only 4000 Japanese troops alive when they finally surrendered, and the Americans had suffered 25 000 casualties.

Okinawa was much bigger. Official American figures put the Japanese losses at over 100 000 and American deaths at 50 000 before it was finally captured in June 1945. If the Japanese could cause such casualties for these islands, how many would die to take Japan itself?

However, there is evidence to suggest that the Japanese were ready to surrender before the atom bomb was dropped. On 13 July the Japanese Foreign Minister, Togo, had contacted his Ambassador in Russia with orders to explore the possibility of peace. Since the Americans had broken the secret Japanese code they knew of this message. Therefore it is possible that the war was about to end without the bomb being dropped. This has led historians to look for other reasons to explain Truman's decision to bomb Hiroshima and Nagasaki. Sources **E** and **F** give two theories.

Why was the bomb dropped?

Source D James Byrnes, US Secretary of State in 1945

> A ny weapon that would bring an end to the war and save a million lives was justified.
>
> From *The Second World War* by Winston Churchill

Source **D** clearly shows that the US Government claimed that the atom bomb was to be dropped to save the lives of Allied troops. The Americans had certainly found it very tough to defeat the Japanese in the Pacific. During 1943 and 1944 the Americans had slowly recaptured the Pacific islands, 'hopping' from one island to the next.

Source E From *A People's History of the United States*, written by Howard Zinn in 1980

> T he Russians had secretly agreed...that they would come into the war [*against Japan*] ninety days after the end of the European war. That turned out to be on 8 May, and so, on 8 August, the Russians were due to declare war on Japan. By then the big bomb would have been dropped...and the Japanese would surrender to the United States, not the Russians, and the United States would be the occupier of post-war Japan.

Source F From *A People's History of the United States*

> T he dropping of the second bomb on Nagasaki seems to have been scheduled [*planned*] in advance and no-one has been able to explain why it was dropped. Was it because this was a plutonium bomb whereas the Hiroshima bomb was a uranium bomb? Were the dead and irradiated of Nagasaki victims of a scientific experiment?

Investigations

1 Look at Source **D**. Why did Byrnes believe it was right to drop the atom bomb?

2 What evidence can you find to support this view?

3 Which sources disagree with Source **D**?

4 Since some sources disagree with Source **D**, does this mean that this source is unreliable? Explain your answer.

5 Why do *you* think that the Americans dropped the atom bomb on Hiroshima? Give your reasons.

8 Depth Study: The soldiers' wars: 1914–45

On the battlefield

> ### How did soldiers feel about going into battle?

The experience of war

The twenty-one years which separate the end of the First World War from the beginning of the Second World War saw some important changes in military technology. Weapons could kill more men, more easily, and more quickly. What is less clear is what changes (if any) took place in the attitudes of the men who fought these wars. Did they become more afraid? Did they hate the enemy more? Did they care less about why they were fighting?

This chapter tries to give some idea of the way the soldiers of the two world wars thought about these issues. In this sense the chapter is the soldiers' story.

On the night before a big battle, soldiers could only think of the next day, as Source **A** reveals.

Source A By a First World War British soldier

> **A**ll through that night I never slept a wink of sleep…I would find myself calculating the chances of survival. Surely a quarter of our number would remain unscathed [*unhurt*]? And the other chances – what are they? Maybe one in three against being killed. One chance in four of being wounded…and one chance in four of being taken prisoner – as good as escaping scot-free.
>
> **Quoted in *Death's Men* by Denis Winter, Penguin 1978**

Source B Death by gas was slow and agonising, but it was rare. Most men recovered. These men, painted by John Singer Sargent from a scene he witnessed in 1918, are suffering from the blinding effects of mustard gas. Why do you think each man has his hand on the shoulder of the man in front?

Christmas 1914

On the other hand, it could not be said that the attitude evident in Source **A** (page 65) was shared by all British soldiers. There was an unofficial truce between the Germans and British during the Christmas of 1914 (Source **C**). The army High Command disapproved of it and details of the truce were not made public until after the war.

Source C   From a British soldier's letter home

You will hardly credit what I am going to tell you: but... listen.

Last night as I sat in my little dug-out...my chum came bursting in...with: 'Bob! Hark at 'em!' And I listened. From the German trenches came the sound of music and singing....

I got up to investigate. Climbing the parapet, I saw a sight which I shall remember to my dying day. Right along the whole of the line were hung paper lanterns...many of them...upon Christmas trees....

...A party of our men got out of their trenches and invited the Germans to meet them halfway and talk. And there in the searchlight they stood. Englishman and German, chatting and smoking cigarettes together midway between the lines.

Quoted in *The Christmas Truce* by M. Brown and S. Seaton, Secker and Warburg 1984

Source D   British and German troops meet in No Man's Land, Christmas 1914

Source E   From an interview with an American soldier, Elliot Johnson, who fought the Germans in 1944

We recognised that we were in a war, but we recognised that they came from families, like we came from families and that they had loved ones, and they were good guys and they were bad guys. We were called on by our government, that our country was in jeopardy [*danger*]. Therefore we had to fight for it. Personally, I had no malice [*hatred*] at any time toward the Germans.

Quoted in *The Good War* by Studs Terkel, Penguin 1984

You can see in Source **D** the barbed wire defences and how close the opposing lines of trenches were to each other. The French did not arrange similar truces with the Germans. Can you suggest why? (Clue: Where was the war being fought?)

The Second World War

Did the British or American soldier of the Second World War hate his German enemy more than in the First World War? Look at Source **E**.

Another American soldier, Ed Lackman, jumped into a ditch in 1944 while fighting in Sicily and found himself face to face with a group of Germans (Source **F**).

Source F By an American soldier, Ed Lackman

There were about five Germans and maybe four or five of us, and we didn't give any thought whatsoever to fighting at first…Then I realised that they had their rifles, we had ours, and then shells were landing and we were cowering against the side of the ditch. The Germans were doing the same thing. And then, the next thing you know there was a lull, we took cigarettes out and we passed 'em round, we were smoking and it's a feeling I cannot describe, but it was a feeling that this was not the time to be shooting at one another…They were human beings, like us. They were just as scared.

Quoted in *Soldiers* by J. Keegan and R. Holmes, Hamish Hamilton 1985

Of course, there were other views as well. A British RAF pilot was asked whether there was any 'chivalry' (respect) between the German and British pilots during the Battle of Britain (Source **G**).

Americans were less generous in their attitude to their Japanese enemies than they were to the Germans. This was partly because of racial and cultural differences. The Japanese would rather die than surrender. This was something American troops found hard to understand.

Was there a change in attitude?

It is impossible to draw any firm conclusions from this evidence. It is true to say that, in general, there were more examples of truces and friendly relations between the two sides on the Western Front in the Great War than there were in the Second World War. But this may be due to the fact that in the First World War the two sides spent much longer in trenches in front of each other and a spirit of 'live and let live' developed. In the Second World War, there was far less time spent in trenches and the periods of combat were more frequent. In these circumstances, it was harder to 'get to know' your enemy.

Remember…

- The attitudes of Allied soldiers to the Germans were much the same in both world wars, although there are more examples of friendly relations in the First World War.

Source G From *The World at War* on Thames Television, 1974

I would say there was no chivalry at all. You mean between the German air force and the British? I'd say absolutely none. Not as far as I was concerned. I hated them. They were trying to do something to us. They were trying to enslave [*make slaves of*] us.

Source H American soldiers with Japanese prisoners of war in 1944

Investigations

1 Why do you think the sinking of the *Lusitania* would have made the soldier in Source **A** on page 65 feel the way he did about the Germans?

2 Which of these sources suggest:
   a) that the British or Americans hated the Germans?
   b) that they did not hate the enemy?
   Quote from each of the sources to support your answer.

3 Can you suggest a reason why the British Army High Command put a stop to any further Christmas truces like the ones in 1914?

4 'These sources prove that the British and American troops in the Second World War did not hate the Germans as much as they did in the First World War'. Do you agree with this view? Remember to back up your answer with evidence from the sources.

'For King and Country'

'Joining up' in the First World War

Britain in 1914 was still a leading world power. Its empire contained 400 million people and 'Empire Day' was celebrated every year. Britons welcomed the war and believed it was necessary to defend the Empire and the British way of life from the 'beastly Hun' (Germany).

In the Great War, the British government produced many posters appealing to people's sense of **patriotism**, to persuade men to volunteer for the army. They appealed to men to fight for their country against the 'Hun' who planned to destroy the British Empire, occupy Britain and enslave its people. 'Honour', 'duty', 'King and Country' were expressions in common use. Men had to be persuaded to join the armed forces because, until 1916, there was no **conscription**. It was up to the individual whether he joined up or not.

Men who did not join the army were made to feel that they were letting the country down at a time when others were playing their part in the war effort. Those out of uniform were often accused of being cowards.

However, there was a strong sense of patriotism in Britain, and the feelings expressed in Source **B** would have been common.

Key words
Patriotism Love of one's country.
Conscription Making it compulsory to join the armed forces.

DESIGNED BY LT. GEN. SIR R. S. S. BADEN POWELL.

Are **YOU** in this?

Source A A First World War recruitment poster

Source B By Harry Parry, a student at Oxford at the time of the Great War. This is what he wrote to his mother explaining why he was going to enlist in the army.

> I have no wish to remain a civilian any longer. Though the idea of war is against my conscience, I feel that in a time of national crisis like the present, I don't have the right to my views if they are against the best interests of the country.

Adapted from *Eye Deep in Hell* by J. Ellis

There were 763 000 volunteers for the British army in the first two months of the Great War. But feelings of patriotism were not the only reason why men flocked to join the army. Some fought to escape from the drudgery of their lives or from poverty and hardship (Source **C**).

Another common reason for joining up in 1914 is given in Source **D**. Britain had not been involved in a war in Europe for 70 years. The chance for some excitement was too much for some lads to resist.

Source C   H. Fellows gives his reasons for joining the Northumberland Fusiliers

B oth my parents were dead, I was very poor and had never had a holiday in my life. When I joined up at Nottingham, I refused the local units and…chose the Northumberland Fusiliers because it gave me the longest train ride.

Quoted in _The First Day on the Somme_ by M. Middlebrook

Source D
By W.H.A. Groom, a soldier in the war

Fighting in the Second World War

By the time the Second World War broke out in 1939 Britain already had conscription. There were no cheering crowds in 1939 to greet the outbreak of war, as there had been in 1914. The British government had tried very hard – perhaps too hard – to avoid another war with Germany. Memories of the last one were still fresh in people's minds.

In the Second World War there was less need for recruitment posters since men had no choice but to join the armed forces. Many posters were designed for a specific purpose – often to boost industrial output or to encourage people to save food.

A military band and marching soldiers are always an inspiring sight, but this was for real – they were off to war and how we youngsters envied them!…And to tell you the truth that was it – glamour, to be in uniform. To take part in a great adventure was as much a reason for so many youths joining up as any sense of patriotism.

From _Poor Bloody Infantry_ by W.H.A. Groom

However, there were, posters which urged men and women to defend Britain, such as the one in Source **E**. Some historians have questioned the success of posters like this one. Not many people from the big cities would have recognised the pleasant village green as part of 'their' Britain.

Source E   A Second World War poster

Your **BRITAIN** · *fight for it now*

American troops were asked the question 'What are we fighting for?' One reply to this question is given in Source **F**.

Source F
An American soldier says what he is fighting for

> Y ou're fighting for your skin on the line. When I enlisted I was as patriotic as all hell. There's no patriotism on the line [*at the front*]. A boy up there 60 days on the line is in danger every minute. He ain't fighting for patriotism.
>
> **From *The American Soldier* by S.A. Stouffer, Princetown University Press 1965**

Many British soldiers also became disillusioned with the war. They no longer believed they were fighting for the same noble reasons they had been fighting for when the war began (Source **G**).

Source G By an anonymous British army captain, from the magazine *The Spectator*, November 1944

> I n short, the British soldier is fighting for the future of the world and does not believe in that future. He is tough, hard, honest and... completely disillusioned. He is not fighting for any ideal – although he hates his enemy and the ways of the enemy – but because he knows that Germany must be utterly [*completely*] defeated before he can get home to his family, his football, his beer and fireside.

Remember...

- **Soldiers in both world wars fought for much the same reasons.**
- **In both wars people felt it was their duty to defend their country.**
- **There was more enthusiasm for war in 1914 than in 1939.**

Investigations

1 Sources **A–G** (pages 68–70) each give at least one reason to explain why men fought in the world wars. Some of the reasons are given in the left-hand column of the table below. Copy out the table in to your book.
a) In the middle column, write the letter of the source where you can find this reason. For example, 'To preserve the British way of life' is the reason in Source **E**, so write 'Source **E**' in the second column next to the reason.
b) In the last column, say whether the source comes from the First or the Second World War. For example, Source **E** comes from the Second World War.

2 Do you think that many men in 1939 would have shared the same enthusiasm for war expressed in Source **D**? (Remember that the Great War was Britain's first war in Europe for 70 years, but 1939 was only 21 years after the end of the last 'Great War'.)

3 Is it possible to say from these sources whether men in the Second World War were *less* patriotic than they were in the Great War? Give reasons for your answer. To answer this, think about:
a) what Sources **D**, **F** and **G** suggest about soldiers' attitudes in the war.
b) whether these three sources provide you with *enough* evidence to make a valid judgment.

Reason for fighting	Found in Source...	Comes from First or Second World War
To stay alive and get home		
To escape from poverty		
To preserve the British way of life	Source E	Second World War
To avoid being thought a coward		
To take part in an adventure		
To support the country in a time of national crisis		

Medical treatment

The Great War wounded

A soldier wounded in a First World War attack faced a grim fate. His pals were not allowed to stop to help him – they had to go on. All men carried an emergency field dressing which they applied to their wound – if they were able. Then they had to wait for the stretcher-bearers. Many wounded men were missed in the chaos and terror of battle and might have to lie for two or three days in No Man's Land before they were found and treated.

If they could, they dragged themselves into a shell-hole, but shell-holes were easier to get into than they were to get out of. Many drowned as the craters filled with rain and mud, unable to claw themselves out.

There was nothing worse for soldiers at the battle front than to hear the cries of their wounded comrades out in No Man's Land and not be able to help them. Death would be slow and painful. Sometimes a truce would be agreed so that each side could collect their dead and wounded without being shot at, or to allow the enemy wounded to be collected from in front of the trenches that had just been attacked. Wounded men who were captured were generally well-treated by each side.

Source A A wounded man is treated in a trench by a Red Cross worker

71

The chances of survival

In the First World War, 13 per cent of men who fought in the British army were killed and 36 per cent were wounded. In the Second World War, of the men who served overseas 5 per cent were killed and 9 per cent were wounded. It would seem, therefore, that there was a much greater chance of becoming a casualty in the 1914–18 war than in the Second World War. At least, that is what these statistics say. In fact, this was not the case.

In the 1939–45 war there were far more people in the army who never went near the fighting. They were involved in non-combat duties. If you include only the men who actually did the fighting in the Second World War, then the figures for killed and wounded would be more like 13 per cent killed and 32 per cent wounded – very similar to the First World War statistics.

The scene described in Source **C** would have been familiar throughout both wars.

The Second World War wounded

Those wounded in the Second World War were not always luckier than those in the Great War. However, they were unlikely to be left untreated for as long as some were in 1914–18, because soldiers were on the move much more in the Second World War.

Medical attention in the First World War was generally close at hand – once the wounded had been brought back – because the trench lines changed so little. Casualty Clearing Stations were permanently in the same place. During the Second World War a Casualty Clearing Station could be 80 miles away and the journey would have to be made in the back of an ambulance.

However, the quality of medical treatment was better and the chances of survival rather more likely than in the First World War. There had been two important medical developments: penicillin and blood transfusions. Penicillin greatly reduced the chances of infection in wounds, and blood transfusions ensured that men no longer died from loss of blood, once they could be treated. Their chances were further improved because it was now possible to take them to a general hospital which could be 250 miles away. Evacuation by plane had not been available to soldiers in the Great War.

Source C A war correspondent describes the scene at a Casualty Clearing Station in France during the First World War

> Men with chunks of steel in their lungs and bowels, vomiting great gobs of blood, men with legs and arms torn from their trunks, men without noses, and their brains throbbing through open scalps, men without faces…

Investigations

1 Why do you think the wounded in the First World War often spent so long in No Man's Land?

2 Can you explain why it was so difficult for wounded men to get out of shell-holes?

3 Why did a First World War soldier, once he had been found, stand a better chance of getting proper medical treatment quickly than a soldier in the 1939–45 war?

4 Why was the quality of medical treatment better in the Second World War?

5 What does the statement 'In the Second World War, of the men who served overseas 5 per cent were killed and 9 per cent were wounded' teach you about the problems of basing your views on statistics?

Remember…

- **Wounded men in the Second World War received better medical treatment but sometimes they had to wait longer to get it.**

9 Depth Study:
The two World Wars and the role of women
Women before the First World War

Women's work in Britain before 1914

Middle and upper-class women before the war were not expected or encouraged to work. There were some types of job which middle-class women could do before they got married. Working as secretaries, or as shop assistants in 'posh' shops was acceptable. Working-class women could also work before they got married. The most typical occupation for women was as domestic servants – cooks or maids – but in the north of England many working-class women worked in factories. Domestic service was considered to be especially suitable for women, because it was good preparation for the job they would do once they got married – being a housewife.

In the case of female workers in the cotton factories of Lancashire, women could stay on to work even after they married or had children, but this was not typical.

If women had to work, they were required to do work which was not physically hard (because, it was thought, women were too 'feeble') or requiring much intelligence (because women were not thought to be as clever as men). But whatever jobs women did before 1914, their work generally had two things in common: they got paid a lot less than men (about half of what men got for doing similar work) and the jobs had no career prospects.

Source A The middle and upper-class woman had a relaxed life-style before the war. For her working-class maid life was not so easy. How can we tell from this picture that the woman in bed must be quite well off?

Women and the First World War

Women's work during the war

It is clear that women found new opportunities during the war. Men were away fighting in the war, so women had to fill the jobs the men had left vacant. Women earned higher wages in these skilled jobs than they had in domestic service or factories before 1914.

The **munitions** industry employed 900 000 women. This work was not popular with middle-class women and it was also harmful to health. But it was well paid – by women's standards – at £3 to £5 a week (a domestic servant was paid £2 a month). These women were nick-named 'munitionettes' and, more seriously, 'canaries'. This was because the chemicals used turned the women's skin yellow.

Other women found jobs in shipyards, on farms, as bus conductors and road sweepers. Much of this was hard, physical and 'unfeminine' work. In many cases they wore trousers. Some of the jobs were renamed to make them sound less like the jobs men had done. So, women road sweepers were called 'street housemaids'!

Women in the war

Once the war had started there was a need for women as nurses to attend the wounded. There had, of course, been women nurses before the war, so this was not new. During the war 23 000 women served as nurses and 15 000 more served as assistants in the Volunteer Aid Detachments (VADs). Many upper and middle-class women VAD workers experienced the grim realities of war. One wrote: 'When I undressed, all my clothes, down to my chemise, reeked of pus'.

Source A Women working as railway porters in the First World War. It was a typical man's job, requiring physical strength, but women coped well enough. This job may also have been renamed to make it sound more 'feminine'. Can you suggest a new name?

FRANCE
ITALY
MALTA
GIBRA
SALON

EGYPT
MESOPOTAMIA
HOLLAND
SWITZERLAND
RUSSIA

V.A.D.
NURSING MEMBERS, COOKS, KITCHEN-MAIDS, CLERKS, HOUSE-MAIDS, WARD-MAIDS, LAUNDRESSES, MOTOR-DRIVERS, ETC:
ARE URGENTLY NEEDED
APPLICATION TO BE MADE TO

Source B Poster advertising for women to join the VADs

Source C   Recruitment poster for the Women's Land Army

Entirely new roles were opened to women. Over 100 000 women served in the various sections of the fighting services: the Women's Army Auxiliary Corps (WAAC), the Women's Royal Naval Service (WRNS), and the Women's Royal Air Force (WRAF). Here they did **non-combatant** jobs such as typists, cooks, cleaners, drivers, and mechanics. This allowed the men who had done these jobs to go to the front to fight. These new services, though, were not set up until the spring of 1917.

The Women's Land Army was also set up in 1917. Its job was to do the farm work that had been done by men now fighting in the war. However, this kind of work was unpopular and only 48 000 women volunteered to fill the 260 000 jobs available.

After the war – back to the sink?

Middle and upper-class women had better career prospects after the war. The Sex Disqualification Removal Act passed in 1919 allowed women to have careers in the civil service and law, although single women could not continue working as teachers or civil servants if they married. However, the percentage of married and single women at work was lower in 1921 than in 1911. In 1920 Oxford University decided to allow women to study for degrees.

However, these changes did not affect working-class women. For them, the only real change was that they were now able to vote. In 1918 the Representation of the People Act allowed women aged 30 and over to vote in elections and in 1928 the Equal Franchise Act lowered the voting age for women to 21 – the same as that for men.

NATIONAL SERVICE
WOMEN'S LAND ARMY

"GOD SPEED THE PLOUGH AND THE WOMAN WHO DRIVES IT"

SERIES W9.

APPLY FOR ENROLMENT FORMS AT YOUR NEAREST POST OFFICE OR EMPLOYMENT EXCHANGE

Investigations

1 Why do you think working-class women were keen to work in the munitions factories?

2 Why were middle-class women not keen to do this kind of work?

3 Why was munitions work harmful?

4 Why would the VAD assistant's clothes have 'reeked of pus'?

5 Which of the non-combatant jobs listed above would have been entirely new for women?

6 Why do you think the Women's Land Army proved so unpopular?

7 Job titles were often changed to make them sound more 'feminine'. There is, however, another possible reason why these jobs were re-named. Can you suggest what it might be? (Clue: What could an employer say if the women demanded equal pay with the men for the same job?)

Key words

Munitions   Industries which were devoted to making ammunitions and weapons for the war.
Non-combatant   Jobs in the armed services which do not involve any fighting.

Women were expected to give up their jobs to men returning from the war. Some accepted this, but many employers did not want to lose their women workers, as their wages were half that of men.

There were also changes in social attitude. Young women in the 1920s, known as 'flappers', shocked many people by wearing short skirts, cutting their hair short, smoking in public and going out without chaperons. This changed the traditional view of how women dressed and behaved.

Source D Women's occupations in 1921

Occupation	Number of women employed
Domestic service (servants, cleaners, cooks)	1 845 000
Textiles (weavers, spinners, lace-makers)	701 000
General workers (shop assistants, factory workers)	688 000
Dress (hat, shoe, wig, glove and corset makers)	602 000
Commerce (clerks, typists)	587 000
Professions (layers, teachers, doctors)	441 000

Adapted from *British Labour Statistics, 1868–1968*, Department of Employment and Productivity

Source E Women in a restaurant in about 1920

Source F The numbers of women and men qualifying as doctors during and after the war

Year	Women	Men
1917	78	539
1918	68	431
1919	99	175
1920	210	374
1921	602	325

Investigations

1 Look back at Source **D** on page 74. Compare the figures for women employed as domestic servants in 1911 with those for 1921 in Source **D** above. What change do you notice?

Here are some possible reasons for this change. Some of these are good explanations and some are not. Write the reasons out and put a tick beside the ones which you think are sensible and a cross against the ones which are think are probably not true.
a) 'There were fewer women domestic servants after the war because more women got married.'
b) 'There were fewer women domestic servants after the war because women could get better paid jobs elsewhere.'
c) 'There were fewer women domestic servants after the war because women wanted to do more dignified work.'

d) 'There were fewer women domestic servants after the war because lots of maids had been killed in the war.'
e) 'There were fewer women domestic servants after the war because women didn't like the uniforms maids had to wear.'

2 How does Source **E** support the view that women were beginning to rebel against old-fashioned attitudes towards them?

3 In the text on page 77 it says that 'Middle and upper-class women had better career prospects after the war'. What evidence can you find in Sources **D** and **F** above and Source **D** on page 74 to support this claim?

Women and the Second World War

How did the Second World War affect the position of women?

The war effort: conscripts and volunteers

At first the government did not want women to help with the war effort. They were told to spend their time on the 'kitchen front'. But the government soon changed its mind and in December 1941 single women between the ages of 18 and 30 were actually conscripted, and could choose whether to serve in the armed services or work in industry. Britain was the only country in the war which made women help with the war effort. Many married women volunteered to do 'war work', such as jobs in factories. Women played a vital role in maintaining factory production.

By 1943 7.5 million women were employed in jobs related to the war. In 1943 there were 1 200 000 more women employed in the engineering, shipbuilding and aircraft industries than before the war. The huge female workforce meant that nurseries had to be set up to look after children. By 1944 there were 1450 nurseries compared to 104 before the war. These were closed down after the war, to help force married women to give up their jobs and go back into the home.

Source A A painting by an official war artist, showing a woman working in an engineering factory in the Second World War

But, as in the First World War, women had proved that they could tackle the most difficult, dangerous and technical of jobs. However, they were still paid much less than men. Winston Churchill rejected a proposal in the 1944 Education Act that women teachers should be paid the same as men, although he allowed them to keep their jobs if they got married.

Women in the armed forces

Two out of every three women conscripted chose to join one of the armed forces rather than work in industry. They joined the ATS (Auxiliary Territorial Services), the WAAF (Women's Auxiliary Air Force), and the WRNS (Women's Royal Naval Service). They had no combat role, but came close in dangerous jobs such as operating anti-aircraft guns, although they were not permitted to actually fire the guns. Women in the WAAF flew aircraft from factories to their RAF bases. The Women's Land Army proved more popular than in the First World War – 80 000 women joined to help maintain vital food supplies by doubling Britain's food output from the 1939 level.

Source B The image of the WRNS on this poster is a smart and glamorous one. The WRNS was the most popular of the armed services open to women, but the jobs in it were not always that exciting (see Source **D**).

WOMEN'S · ROYAL · NAVAL · SERVICE

join the Wrens
AND · FREE · A · MAN · FOR · THE · FLEET

APPLY TO DIRECTOR W.R.N.S. ADMIRALTY S.W.I.
OR THE NEAREST EMPLOYMENT EXCHANGE

Source C A number of the world's first all-woman 93rd Searchlight Regiment. They proved very capable operators in a dangerous job. German bombers would dive down the beam with their machine guns blazing in an effort to smash the lights.

Source D Join the Navy and see the world! These members of the ATS are preparing vegetables. What do you think would have been their opinion of the WRNS poster (Source **B**)?

Source E Mona Marshall, a nursemaid before the war and a steelworker during it, was clear about how the war affected women

To be honest, the war was the best thing that ever happened to us. I was as green as grass and terrified if anyone spoke to me. I had been brought up not to argue. My generation [*of women*] had been taught to do as we were told. At work you did exactly as your boss told you and you went home to do exactly as your husband told you. The war changed all that. The war made me stand on my own two feet.

Quoted in *The People's War* by Peter Lewis, 1986

After the war

The divorce rate in 1945 was one divorce for every hundred marriages – five times more than the 1939 rate. (Today it is one in every three!) Couples had spent so much time apart during the years of the war that they were strangers when they finally got back together again (Source **F**). Both the men and the women had been changed by their very different experiences of the war, and the women found it especially hard to get used to the role of staying at home, after the relative freedom that they had experienced during the war years (Source **G**).

Source F   One woman's memory of married life after the war

> **A**fter a while we settled to some sort of married life, but there were times when I thought that if there was a hell on earth, I was living it.

Source G   In 1946 a book called *Living Together Again*, by a doctor and his wife, tried to help men and women put their lives back together again. It suggested that many women would not welcome going back to the old way of things before the war.

> **M**any will also feel that they are going back to prison, unless they have some life away from the sinks and brooms and washtubs.
>
> **From *Living Together Again* by P. and L. Bendit, 1946**

Remember...

- Both wars opened up new job opportunities for women.

- Women learned new skills and became more confident of their abilities.

- After both wars women found themselves forced back into standard 'women's jobs'.

- Women were still some way from equality with men, but both wars had brought that aim a little closer.

Investigations

1 Why was being a searchlight operator a dangerous job?

2 Why might some women have been unhappy with the duties carried out by the Wren in Source **D**?

3 What do you suppose the authors in Source **G** meant by the term 'prison'?

4 Which of the two jobs shown in Source **C** and Source **D** would Mona Marshall (in Source **E**) have preferred to do? Give reasons for your answer.

5 What does Source **G** suggest that women wanted from their lives after the war?

6 Can you think why closing down the wartime nurseries after the Second World War forced many married women to go back to being housewives?

7 Why do you think so many wartime marriages ended in divorce once the war was over? (Clue: Think especially about how the war had changed the attitudes of women. Look at Source **E** on page 80 as well.)

8 Copy the table below into your files or exercise book. The column on the left contains four statements about how the two wars affected the position of women.
a) In the second column you should write whether you agree with the statement or not.
b) In the last column you must give the evidence you have for your view. To do this, make use of the text and sources in this chapter.

Statement	I agree/I disagree with this statement	My evidence from the text and sources is...
'Women did more dangerous jobs in the Second World War than in the First World War'		
'Women's self-confidence increased as a result of their wartime roles in both wars'		
'Women did more important jobs in the First World War than in the Second World War'		
'Women were happy to go back to being housewives after the Second World War'		

10 The post-war world
The Cold War

Why did the Cold War start?

"An iron curtain has descended"

In 1945 the USA and the Soviet Union had been allies, but the only thing they had in common was the need to defeat Germany. When the war was over they became very suspicious of one another.

Source A Europe and the 'Iron Curtain'

The 'Iron Curtain'

NATO members (Greece and Turkey joined in 1952; West Germany joined in 1955)

Communist Countries

Neutral Communist Country

Yugoslavia, although Communist, refused to be dominated by Russia, and so was not behind the Iron Curtain

Stalin had seen Russia invaded from the West twice in the past 40 years. He was determined that it would not happen again. At the end of the war the countries of Eastern Europe were occupied by 12 million Soviet troops. Stalin wanted to create a buffer zone to protect the Soviet Union.

One by one the countries of eastern Europe were brought under Soviet control. By March 1947 the buffer zone was fully in place. In March 1946 the former British Prime Minister Winston Churchill had declared 'An iron curtain has descended across the continent'.

The Marshall Plan

The USA regarded Russia's motives with deep suspicion. They feared that Communism was going to spread across the world. In 1947 President Truman announced that the USA would help any country that wanted protection against Communism. In that year the USA gave help to Greeks who were fighting Communists in their country. Later America would try and stop Communism spreading into Korea (see pages 85 and 86) and Vietnam.

In Europe, Truman was afraid that the war had caused such hardship that people would turn to Communism. Therefore, in 1947 the USA introduced the Marshall Plan. Over the next three years almost 14 billion dollars of American aid was given to European countries to help feed the people and rebuild industry destroyed by the war. Britain got the most – 3 billion dollars. Stalin refused to allow the countries of Eastern Europe to apply for Marshall Aid. He believed that it was an American plot to take control of Europe.

Suspicion between the two **Superpowers** had turned into hostility. This hostility was called the Cold War and was to continue until the collapse of the Soviet Union in 1991. The Superpowers were each determined to stop the other increasing their power.

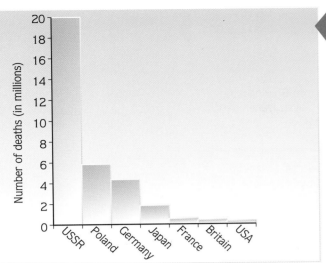

Source C   Stalin's reply to Churchill's 'Iron Curtain' speech

T he following circumstances should not be forgotten. The Germans made their invasion of the USSR through Finland, Poland, Romania, Bulgaria and Hungary…The Soviet Union's loss of life has been several times greater than that of Britain and the United States put together. And so what can be surprising about the fact that the Soviet Union, anxious for its future safety, is trying to see to it that governments loyal to the Soviet Union should exist in those countries.

A t the present moment in world history nearly every nation must choose between alternative ways of life. One way is based upon the will of the majority, free elections, individual liberty, freedom of speech and religion. The second way of life is based upon the will of a minority forcibly imposed upon the majority. It relies on terror and oppression…I believe that it must be the policy of the United States to support free peoples who are resisting subjugation [domination] by armed minorities or outside pressure.

Source D   President Truman speaking to the US Congress in March 1947

Source E   A West German cartoon from about 1950

The nuclear threat

By 1949 the Soviet Union had developed their own atomic bomb. In the same year the countries of Western Europe joined with the USA to form NATO (North Atlantic Treaty Organization), an alliance to defend themselves from Russian attack. Both sides became involved in a race to produce new and more powerful weapons. In 1954 the USA exploded a hydrogen bomb, more powerful than the atom bomb. The next year Russia followed suit. In 1957 the Soviet Union developed the Intercontinental Ballistic Missile (ICBM) which could send a nuclear warhead over huge distances at high speed. In 1958 the Americans produced their own ICBM. In 1962 a crisis arose that brought the world to the brink of nuclear war.

Investigations

1 What point is Truman making in Source **D**?

2 How does Source **B** help to explain Stalin's view in Source **C**?

3 Look at Sources **B**, **C** and **D**. How well do they explain why a Cold War developed between the USA and the Soviet Union? To answer this question consider:
   a) What causes of the Cold War are mentioned?
   b) What causes are not mentioned?

4 Look at Source **E**. The prisoners are Poland, Czechoslovakia, Hungary, Romania and Bulgaria. The banner says 'Thanks to our liberators'.
   a) What point is the cartoonist trying to make?
   b) Does Source **E** agree with the views in Source **C** or Source **D**? Explain your answer.

Key words

Superpowers   At the start of the twentieth century there had been a number of powerful countries (see Chapter 1, Source A). They had been known as the 'Great Powers'. At the end of The Second World War their were two countries – the USA and the USSR –who were far more powerful than the rest, and so were called the 'Superpowers'.

The Cuban Missile Crisis

Cuba is an island in the Caribbean, just south of the United States. Most Cubans were very poor, working on sugar plantations. In 1959 the government of Cuba was overthrown by revolutionaries led by Fidel Castro. Castro took land from the rich, many of whom were Americans, and gave it to the Cuban peasants. The USA reacted by not buying Cuban sugar.

Castro was not a Communist but was forced to turn to the Soviet Union for help. In April 1961 America backed an invasion of Cuba, in the Bay of Pigs, by Cubans opposed to Castro. This invasion failed, but it convinced Castro that the USA was his enemy, and in December 1961 he declared Cuba a Communist country.

In October 1962 US spy planes saw missile bases being built on Cuba. The missiles were on Soviet ships heading towards Cuba. The USA was under threat from Russian missiles launched from Cuba. US President Kennedy ordered a blockade of Cuba. No ships would be allowed in or out. The world held its breath as the Russian ships continued to head for Cuba. Would they turn round or would war break out between the Superpowers? The Russians sent Kennedy two letters. One demanded that the Americans back down, while the other offered to withdraw the missiles if America promised not to invade Cuba. Kennedy agreed not to invade, and the Russian ships turned round. The crisis was over. Cuba has remained Communist even after the collapse of the Soviet Union.

Détente

The Cuban Missile Crisis had frightened everyone, including the Superpowers. Immediately afterwards they set up a direct telephone link

Source F The importance of Cuba and its position in relation to the USA

Source G Khruschev, the Soviet leader, writing in 1964

We were quite sure that the Americans would never accept a Communist Cuba. We had to find a really effective way to stop American interference in the Caribbean area. The logical answer was missiles…We had no desire to start a war. We sent a letter to the Americans saying that we agreed to move our missiles as long as the President promised that there would be no invasion of Cuba. Finally Kennedy gave in and agreed to such a promise. It was a great victory for us.

Source H A modern American account of the crisis

At the end of two weeks, Kennedy, faced with two letters from Khruschev giving conflicting replies, chose to answer the more acceptable one. Russia agreed to remove all offensive weapons…if the United states promised not to invade Cuba; the President agreed and the crisis was over…Kennedy had won the war of nerves.

From *A concise history of the American Republic* by Morrison, Commager and Leuchtenberg

between the White House in Washington and the Kremlin in Moscow. This was called the Hotline. Although the two sides were still enemies it was not in either of their interests for war to break out. In the 1970s and 1980s this more relaxed approach became known as Détente. Both sides met regularly and sorted out problems.

For 30 years the Berlin Wall was the symbol of the Cold War. It was built in 1961 by the Russians to prevent people leaving the Russian sector of Berlin. In 1990 this symbol of Soviet power was demolished. The Cold War really was over.

Investigations

1 Why did a nuclear war seem likely during the Crisis?

2 Look at Source **G**. How was Khruschev able to claim that he had won?

3 Look at Source **H**. How were the Americans able to claim that they had won?

4 Who do you think won? Explain your answer.

Remember...

- **The Second World War produced two Superpowers – the USA and the Soviet Union.**

- **The Cold War between the two Superpowers was caused by their suspicion of each other's motives. They also had the weapons to destroy one another.**

The United Nations

- **Why was the UN created?**
- **How successful has it been?**

Source A   How the UN is organised

The Secretary-General
- Appointed by a majority vote of the General Assembly.
- In charge of the staff who work for the UN.
- In charge of relief when there is a disaster in the world.

The General Assembly
- All member countries attend.
- Meets once a year.

Military Staff Committee
- Gives advice on military intervention.
- The 5 permanent members of the Security Council are represented.

The Economic and Social Council
- Has 27 members elected by the General Assembly.
- In charge of the UN's work in achieving its aims for economic and social well-being in the world.

The Security Council
- Tries to stop war.
- Can order troops into a member country to 'keep the peace'.
- 5 permanent members: Britain, China, France, USA and Russia. All 5 must agree for an action to be taken.
- Originally 6 other members, though this has now been increased to 10. These places are taken by member nations, each taking a turn.

The origins of the United Nations

Over eight million soldiers had died in the First World War and 50 million people died in the Second. Something had to be done to make sure that in future countries worked together to prevent war. On 25 June 1945, 51 countries met in San Francisco to sign the Charter of the United Nations.

There were two main aims. In its own words these were:

- 'To save succeeding generations from the scourge of war, which twice in our lifetime has brought untold sorrow to mankind.'
- To promote 'the economic and social advancement of all people.'

Ending the scourge of war: Korea

The UN first used a peace-keeping force in 1950, during the crisis in Korea, a peninsula on the northeast coast of China. From 1910 until 1945 it had been a colony of Japan. After the defeat of Japan in the Second World War, the Russians and the Americans agreed to temporarily divide Korea into two zones – North and South. In 1947 the UN tried to hold elections so that the Korean people could decide who should rule Korea. The Russians refused to allow the UN into their Northern Zone. Instead, a Communist government was set up led by Kim Il Sung, who was to rule there until his death in 1994.

Source B   US tanks fire on Chinese troops in Korea, 1951

In 1950 the Communists in the North invaded the South. The UN ordered the North to withdraw. The North Koreans refused and quickly conquered the South, until only a small area around Pusan remained under Southern control. Troops from 16 countries made up the UN forces, but 50 per cent of the land forces and 93 per cent of the air forces came from the USA, as did the overall commander of the UN forces, General MacArthur. UN troops pushed the Northern army back to the old border, the '38th parallel'. Source **C** explains what followed. After three years of warfare the border remained unchanged.

CHINA

N. KOREA

38th parallel

Seoul

S. KOREA

Pusan

North Korean invasion begins June 1950. UN forces counter attack nearly to the Chinese border by November 1950.

By September 1950 only a small area in the South holds out against North Korean troops

CHINA

July 1951

38th parallel

January 1951

November 1950. China invades Korea and pushes back UN forces

UN forces advance north to the 38th parallel. Stalemate. Border between North and South remains unchanged.

N. Korean forces

UN forces

Chinese forces

Source C Map of the Korean War

Source D Nowadays all UN vehicles, even tanks, are painted white so they can be easily seen. This helps to show that they are not an offensive force but are there to stop the fighting.

Peacekeeping since Korea

Since the Korean War the UN has adopted a different policy towards peace-keeping. Whenever there is a crisis, the role of the UN troops is to stop the opposing sides from fighting, and not to take sides or fire, unless in self-defence. The UN's tanks and equipment are painted white so that they stand out clearly. In this peace-keeping role the UN's forces are often heavily outnumbered and this is a problem unless the two sides agree to stop fighting. For instance, in 1994 the UN had to leave the African country of Rwanda and allow civil war to break out between the Hutu and Tutsi tribes because it did not have enough troops to stop them fighting. Hundreds of thousands of Rwandans died in the war that followed.

Has the UN succeeded in ending the 'scourge of war'?

There has been a war somewhere in the world every year since the end of the Korean War. Therefore you could say that the UN has failed. However, it is perhaps impossible to end war itself. There has been no world war since 1945, and in this respect the UN can claim to have been a success.

Investigations

1 Look at Source **B** on page 85 and the text. What evidence can you find to suggest that it was the USA rather than the UN which was in control of the anti-Communist troops in Korea?

2 Look at Source **D** on page 83. How does this help to explain why the USA wanted to defeat the Communist government in North Korea?

3 How successful were the UN in preventing 'the scourge of war' in Korea? Explain your answer.

Economic and social advancement

Refugees

The Second World War produced millions of refugees who were forced to flee from their home to escape from the fighting, or whose home had been destroyed. There were 20 million in Europe alone. This was such a huge problem that the UN relief agency (UNRRA) was set up in 1943, two years before the UN itself. It spent £600 million over the next six years, most of it given by the USA. By the mid 1950s the refugee problem in Europe had mainly been solved but there have been so many wars and natural disasters since 1945 that the UN High Commission for Refugees has been dealing with huge numbers of refugees ever since. For instance in 1994 the civil war in Rwanda led to millions of Rwandans fleeing to the neighbouring countries of Tanzania and Zaire, where they had to be fed and sheltered.

Health

The agency which has the job of improving the world's health is the WHO, the World Heath Organisation. It has done much to help wipe out disease. In 1980 it announced that the world was free of smallpox. This disease had once killed 2 million people a year. In 1985 it reported that on average people were living 20 years longer than they had in 1950.

Education, science and culture

The UN agency responsible for education, science and culture is called UNESCO (United Nations Educational, Scientific, and Cultural Organization). It has led a campaign to help people in poorer countries to read and write. In 1970 only 10 per cent of Ethiopians could read and write. Now the figure is over 70 per cent. UNESCO was also responsible for organising a massive international campaign to save the temples of Ancient Egypt from destruction when the new High Dam was built at Aswan (Source **F**).

Source F The Temple of Philae. In the 1960s it had to be moved stone by stone to a new site, above the water level of Lake Nasser.

In 1977 UNESCO tried to shift control of television, radio and newspapers away from the richer countries. The richer countries feared that the governments in poorer countries just wanted to censor the news. In 1984 Britain withdrew from UNESCO and America followed the next year. They felt that it spent too much money on political issues. Together they had contributed over 25 per cent of UNESCO's funds.

Source E Refugees from the Rwandan civil war, 1994

Investigations

- **The UN has survived the Cold War. There has not been a world war in the last 50 years.**
- **There are now 157 member countries of the UN.**

Remember...

1 What evidence can you find here to support the view that the UN has succeeded in its aim of improving the economic and social condition of the world?

2 What evidence can you find to suggest that the UN still has much to achieve?

The Space Race

'We have the technology'

By September 1944 German scientists had developed the V2 rocket (Source **A**) and 1000 of these were to fall on the south-east of England before the Second World War was over. With the beginning of the Cold War both the USA and the USSR set out to produce rockets which could carry nuclear warheads. It was not just the German technology which they were both using, but also the German scientists. Werner von Braun, who had designed the V2, went to work in America along with many of his team.

The race to the moon

Ordinary Americans were convinced that the USA was the number one country in the world. They had won the war and they enjoyed a standard of living that was far higher than anywhere else. This certainty was shattered on 4 October 1957, when the Soviet Union launched the first ever satellite, Sputnik, into space. The Cold War was still at its height. It was now a matter of honour for the USA to overtake the Russians. The Space Race had begun. In 1961 President Kennedy officially announced the finishing post (Source **B**). It would be a race to the moon.

Source A   A German V2 rocket in the Imperial War Museum, London. This could deliver an explosive warhead onto an English city and was too fast to be caught by a plane.

I believe that this nation should commit itself to achieving a goal, before this decade is out, of landing a man on the moon and returning him safely to earth. No single space project will be more exciting, or more impressive to mankind.

Quoted in *Purnell History of the Twentieth Century*, BPC

Source B   US President Kennedy, May 1961

Source C   On 12 April 1961 the Russian Yuri Gagarin orbited the earth once in his spacecraft, Vostok 1

Source D The race into space

At first the Soviet Union appeared to be well in the lead, especially in April 1961 when they astounded the world by sending the first man into space. Overnight, Yuri Gagarin became a world famous name. Two years and two months later the Soviet Union scored another success when Valentina Tereshkova became the first woman in space. In fact, the Americans were probably already in the lead.

The American spacecraft were far more advanced than their Soviet counterparts, which is why they were taking longer to develop. However, it was in the interests of NASA, the National Aeronautics and Space Administration, to give the impression that they thought the Russians were ahead. Then the US government would spend still more money on the space programme. In the end it cost them 25 billion dollars. Watched by an astonished world, live on their TV screens, Neil Armstrong and Buzz Aldrin left Apollo 11 and landed on the surface of the moon on 20 July 1969. The USA had won the Space Race.

After the race

Space travel did not end with Apollo 11. There were more Apollo missions to the moon and the Russians landed an unmanned lunar rover, Lunakhod. The Soviet Union concentrated on developing their Mir space station while NASA produced the reusable Space Shuttle which could land back on earth, unlike all previous rockets. The emphasis was now on scientific and military research. The public were no longer fascinated by space now that the race was over. Space exploration was no longer in the news.

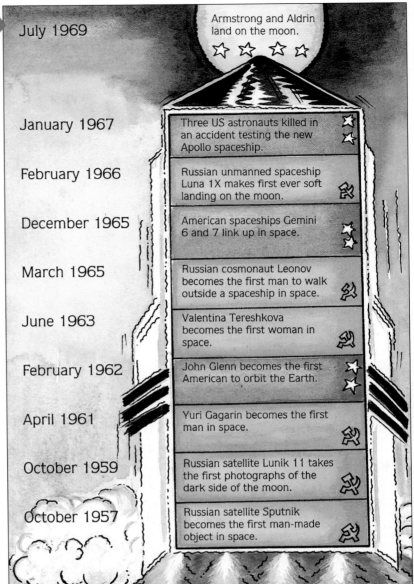

July 1969	Armstrong and Aldrin land on the moon.
January 1967	Three US astronauts killed in an accident testing the new Apollo spaceship.
February 1966	Russian unmanned spaceship Luna 1X makes first ever soft landing on the moon.
December 1965	American spaceships Gemini 6 and 7 link up in space.
March 1965	Russian cosmonaut Leonov becomes the first man to walk outside a spaceship in space.
June 1963	Valentina Tereshkova becomes the first woman in space.
February 1962	John Glenn becomes the first American to orbit the Earth.
April 1961	Yuri Gagarin becomes the first man in space.
October 1959	Russian satellite Lunik 11 takes the first photographs of the dark side of the moon.
October 1957	Russian satellite Sputnik becomes the first man-made object in space.

Source E Buzz Aldrin on the moon

Remember...

- **The Space Race was part of the Cold War rivalry between the Superpowers – America and the Soviet Union.**

Investigations

1 Why did the USA and the USSR want the German rocket scientists?

2 Read Source **B**.
   a) According to President Kennedy, why did America want to land a man on the moon?
   b) What other reasons do you think that there might have been which Kennedy does not mention?

89

Reconstruction

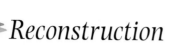

- **Why did the losers of the Second World War become so successful in the years that followed?**
- **Why did Britain fail to keep pace with Germany and Japan?**

Source A
Tokyo in 1945

By 1945 the war was over, but large areas lay in ruins. Germany and Japan had seen many of their cities destroyed, leaving millions homeless and industry in ruins. Yet today Japan and Germany are economic superpowers. Why is this?

Source B
Tokyo today

Source C
GNP (Gross National Product) per head in 1985

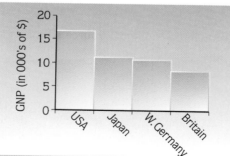

giving 2 billion dollars to help rebuild Japan. There were two reasons for this:
- The USA feared that the Japanese would turn to Communism if they remained poor.
- A prosperous Japan would buy lots of American goods.

To solve the food crisis land was taken from the rich and sold to the peasants at very low prices. Now, the harder the peasants worked the more they could earn. With their profit they would buy goods from Japanese factories, which helped industry to grow.

There was no doubt that Japan had caused the war in the Pacific. In future they promised to have only a small self-defence force which could not be used to attack other countries. While Britain and America continued to spend millions on nuclear weapons, Japan invested the money in modern factories and industry.

Japan

It was not just Hiroshima and Nagasaki that had been destroyed. Conventional bombs had also flattened other Japanese cities such as Tokyo, where as many as 100 000 people may have been killed. Japan had no oil and little food and 13 million Japanese were out of work. Disaster beckoned.

Just as in Europe with the Marshall Plan (see page 82), it was the USA who provided the money,

Key words

GNP GNP is Gross National Product, that is the total wealth produced by a country. If you divide this figure by the number of people living in a country you get the GNP per head. This gives you an idea as to how wealthy the people are and how efficient their economy is.
Free trade When two or more countries agree to remove customs barriers to trade between them.

Japan has very few raw materials and so has to import them. This means that goods made in Japan should be more expensive than goods made elsewhere. The Japanese overcame this problem by concentrating on high technology industries. Today Japan produces 25 per cent of the world's cars and 90 per cent of video recorders.

The French, British and American zones were united in 1949 to form the Federal Republic of Germany (West Germany). The Marshall Plan quickly helped to rebuild German industry.

Berlin was divided into four sectors, just like Germany. In 1949 Russia blocked all the land routes into Berlin. It wanted Berlin to become part of the Soviet sector. The US airlifted food supplies and Russia backed down.

Russia stripped their zone, taking machinery and raw materials to help repair the war damage done to Soviet industry by the Germans

British Zone

Russian Zone

French Zone

American Zone

Berlin

Frankfurt

Germany

Germany was in such a terrible condition at the end of the war that the first year was known as 'Year Zero'. Millions were homeless and refugees had fled west fleeing from either Nazi terror or the advancing Red Army of the Soviet Union, which sought to punish all Germans for the millions of Russians killed in the war.

American money from the Marshall Plan helped rebuild German factories. New machinery and workers desperate for work allowed these factories to be very efficient. In 1957 West Germany helped to create the European Economic Community (EEC).

Remember...

- Japan and Germany were able to build new and modern factories. Britain continued to use old ones.
- Britain received more Marshall Aid than either Germany or Japan.
- Britain had nuclear weapons and large numbers of troops. Germany and Japan had neither.

Investigations

1 Look at Source **E**.
   a) Why did Britain spend more on defence than Japan?
   b) How far does this explain why the Japanese performance in Source **C** is better than Britain's?

   To answer this you will need to read this unit and find any other factors which can explain Source **C**. Then decide whether defence is more or less important than these factors.

2 Look at the German figures in Source **C**. Are the reasons why they have performed better than Britain the same as those for Japan, or are there different reasons? Explain your answer.

This gradually introduced free trade between the original six members and so gave German industry a market of over 180 million people, bigger even than the USA. West Germany became the most powerful economy in Europe. In 1990 the two halves of Germany were once more united.

Britain

At the end of the war the British economy was in a bad way. Britain owed 3 billion pounds to other countries. Britain was a country that relied on trade, but the war had greatly reduced the amount of world trade.

There was no money to invest in new factories, and so machinery which had been out of date before the war continued to be used.

Britain turned down the chance to join the EEC in 1957. Britain did not want to be just a part of Europe, but a world power. Britain wanted to continue to import cheap food from its Commonwealth countries such as Canada, New Zealand and Australia. To make matters worse, Britain's status as a power required the maintenance of modern weapons, large armed forces and even nuclear weapons.

Although the British economy did grow in the 1950s and 1960s, it grew much less quickly than that of other countries.

Source E
Defence spending in 1979 as a percentage of Gross National Product

Britain 5.4 per cent

Japan 1 per cent

Depth Study: The end of Empire

- **Why did the European countries build Empires?**
- **Who benefited from these Empires?**
- **Why did these Empires collapse after the Second World War?**

The European Empires

In the eighteenth and nineteenth centuries the countries of Europe had built huge Empires around the world. The most important reasons for this were:

- To make themselves wealthy. Colonies often had important raw materials which were taken back to the factories in Europe and turned into manufactured goods which could then be sold around the world.
- Building an Empire became a patriotic duty, to prove that your country was superior.
- Taking control of a colony to stop someone else doing so.
- Many people believed that they were bringing a better quality life to the people of the Empire.

By 1939 more than 25 per cent of people in the world lived in parts of the European Empires. Yet just 30 years after the end of the Second World War those Empires had almost completely disappeared. Why had this happened? There were two main reasons:

- The Second World War had cost so much money that countries like Britain were seriously in debt and could no longer afford to defend a world-wide Empire.
- The people of the Empires did not want to be ruled by Europeans. At the end of the First World War many small countries in Europe, such as Czechoslovakia, had been allowed to rule themselves. The people of the Empires wanted the same thing.

The British Empire

The British Empire was the biggest of the European Empires. In the 1920s and 30s it had made part of its Empire into a Commonwealth. Huge countries, like Canada, Australia and New Zealand, had quite small populations dominated by white settlers. They were allowed to rule themselves as independent countries, but with the King of England as the Head of State. They were called dominions. South Africa

was allowed to become a dominion, even though the ruling White settlers were only a small minority of the population, and the Black people were given no say in the running of their own country.

India

India was the 'Jewel in the Crown' of the British Empire. It was the richest colony, with an enormous population, far greater than that of Britain. The Indian people wanted to rule themselves, but Britain refused to treat them like Canada or Australia.

Source A   Sir W. Joynson-Hicks, British Home Secretary, 1928

> We did not conquer India for the benefit of the Indians...We conquered India as a market for the goods of Great Britain.

Between the two world wars Mahatma Gandhi became the leader of the Indian independence movement. He wanted to use non-violent methods to force the British to grant India independence. He organised strikes and huge protest meetings as well as campaigns to **boycott** British goods and to stop paying taxes. Faced with these nationwide protests the British allowed the provinces of India to have their own elected governments, but they would not grant independence.

The war changed everything. The Japanese overran much the of the British Empire in Asia and threatened to capture India. The Indian Congress Party refused to support Britain in the war, so the British promised them independence once the war was over if they would join in the war against Japan. In 1947 Britain gave up control of India. However, the Hindus and Muslims wanted to rule themselves, and so two separate countries were formed, India and Pakistan. There were terrible riots which left as many as one million dead and led to ten million people becoming refugees.

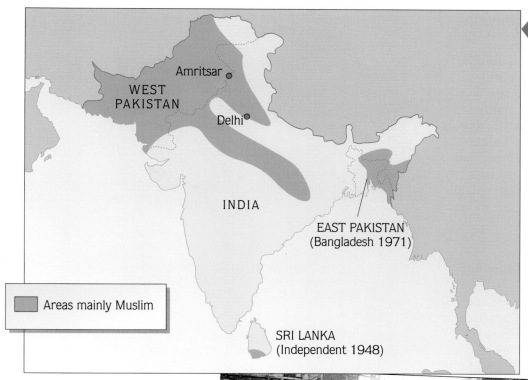

Source B Map of India showing the main Muslim and Hindu areas

WEST PAKISTAN

Amritsar

Delhi

INDIA

EAST PAKISTAN
(Bangladesh 1971)

SRI LANKA
(Independent 1948)

Areas mainly Muslim

Source C Mohammed Jinnah, the leader of the Muslim League, speaking in 1943

The Muslims believe in a single god and the Hindus worship idols...They consider cows sacred – we want to eat them.

Source D Amritsar in 1947, after rioting between Hindus and Muslims

Key words

Boycott To refuse to buy goods, as a means of putting on pressure.

Investigations

1 a) Find three reasons why European countries built Empires.
b) Which one does Source **A** suggest is the most important?
c) Do you believe that Source **A** is reliable evidence about the British government's motives in India? Give your reason.

2 Look at Sources **B**, **C** and **D**.
a) What problems did the British face when granting independence to India?
b) What problems would still exist for the new governments of India and Pakistan?

Africa

Even though India was granted independence in 1947, Britain and the other European countries were still unwilling to give up their African colonies. Africa was seen differently.

In 1873 there had been no European colonies in Africa south of the Sahara except South Africa and the Portuguese colonies. By 1900 the continent was divided up by the Europeans, as shown in Source **E**. Why was this?

● As we saw earlier, the Europeans wanted to exploit the raw materials to be found in the colonies.

● The Europeans wanted to bring an end to the slave trade.

● Many British people believed that they were building an Empire with peace and justice for the benefit of the African people. People believed that if left to themselves the African tribes would fight one another.

Kenya

To see how the British Empire worked we will look at one colony – Kenya – as an example. In the early years of the twentieth century the British government decided to encourage British people to settle in Kenya. Much of the land was taken from the native people and sold cheaply to the new settlers.

After the Second World War the leaders of the largest tribe, the Kikuyu, demanded independence for Kenya. Men such as Jomo Kenyatta and Chief Koinange hoped to use peaceful means to persuade the British. Others were less patient. Between 1952 and 1956 there was an uprising by Kenyan natives known as the Mau Mau, in which a number of White settlers were murdered. There was also violence against other Africans – violence which British rule was meant to have ended. Kenyatta and other moderate leaders were imprisoned for being involved in the Mau Mau, despite a lack of evidence against them. In 1959 Kenyatta was released. But by now everything had changed. Britain could no longer afford to keep its Empire and in 1963 Kenya became one of the independent countries in the British Commonwealth. Kenyatta became its first Prime Minister. The following year Kenya became a republic with Kenyatta as its President.

Source E The scramble for Africa

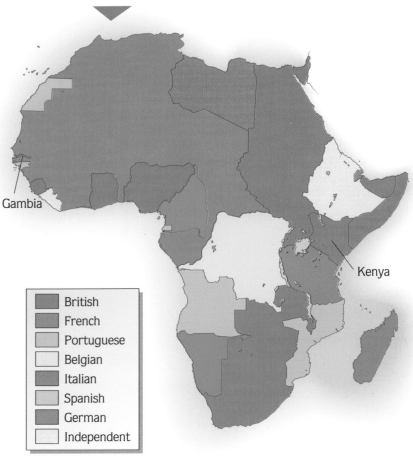

British
French
Portuguese
Belgian
Italian
Spanish
German
Independent

Gambia

Kenya

Source F Sir Harry Johnstone, a White settler, speaking of the highlands of Kenya at the start of the century

I am able to say that here we have a territory admirably suited for a White man's country, and I can say that with no thought of injustice to any native race...This will be one source of profit to the United Kingdom.

Quoted in *Kenyatta* by Dennis Murray-Brown, Allen and Unwin 1972

Source G Richard Meinertzhagen, reporting a conversation with the British Governor of Kenya in 1902

He [*the governor*] intends to confine the natives to reserves and use them as cheap labour on the farms. I suggested that the country belonged to the Africans and that their interests must prevail...He would not have it; he kept on using the word **paramount** with reference to the claims of Europeans. I said that some day the Africans would be educated and armed; that there would be a clash.

From *Kenya Diary 1902–6* by Richard Meinertzhagen